DANGEROUS FIELDWORK

CO-AKQ-821

RAYMOND M. LEE
Royal Holloway University of London

Qualitative Research Methods
Volume 34

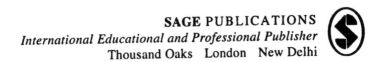

SAGE PUBLICATIONS
International Educational and Professional Publisher
Thousand Oaks   London   New Delhi

For information address:

SAGE Publications, Inc.
2455 Teller Road
Thousand Oaks, California 91320

SAGE Publications Ltd.
6 Bonhill Street
London EC2A 4PU
United Kingdom

SAGE Publications India Pvt. Ltd.
M-32 Market
Greater Kailash I
New Delhi 110 048 India

Printed in the United States of America

Library of Congress Cataloging-in-Publication Data

Lee, Raymond M.
　　Dangerous fieldwork / Raymond M. Lee.
　　　　p.　　cm. — (Qualitative research methods; v. 34)
　　Includes bibliographical references.
　　ISBN 0-8039-5660-6 (cl). — ISBN 0-8039-5661-4 (pb)
　　1. Ethnology—Fieldwork.　2. Ethnologists—Social conditions.
　　3. Ethnologists—Psychology.　4. Ethnologists—Health and hygiene.
　　I. Title.　II. Series
　　GN346.L44　1995
　　305.8—dc20
　　　　　　　　　　　　　　　　　　　　　　　　　　　　　　94-33266

95　96　97　98　99　10　9　8　7　6　5　4　3　2　1

Sage Project Editor: Susan McElroy

To Tom McGlew

CONTENTS

SERIES EDITORS' INTRODUCTION

Fieldworkers are often quick to deny, qualify, or dismiss any "Indiana Jones" or danger-seeking imagery that others may attribute to their trade. Yet, romantic disclaimers aside, a good number of field studies in both sociology and anthropology place even the most timid and retiring of fieldworkers in settings and situations that are potentially dangerous to their health and safety. Any list of potential dangers is likely to be lengthy, but a short list would surely include the hazards of assault, rape, and robbery; the risks of infection, accident, and disease; the possibilities of arrest, harassment, verbal abuse, and violent confrontation. To stay out of harm's way requires caution, of course, but caution is a matter that rests in part on the cultural knowledge about how and where danger is likely to arise in particular social situations. Since such knowledge is an aim rather than a resource for fieldworkers, understanding and thus minimizing the risky elements of the trade is an emergent, unpredictable, and setting-specific matter.

Nevertheless, a good deal of wisdom and lore is passed back and forth among social researchers as to how best to cope with both the ambient and the situational dangers experienced in the field. Little of it is formalized, however, and most of it is exchanged through the confessional accounts, corridor talks, and war stories that animate a given research community. This ongoing cautionary conversation about how danger is managed (or mismanaged) in the field is marked by a curious mix of sound advice, media-influenced exaggeration, fatalistic glossings, and engaging tales of living dangerously—but safely—behind the lurk lines of conflict, violence, and duress.

Raymond Lee, in this 34th volume of the Sage Qualitative Research Methods Series, is out to influence and perhaps alter this conversation. *Dangerous Fieldwork* is a careful yet compact treatment of the risks of social research, as carried out in situations that are, on the surface, anything but researcher-friendly. Drawing on his own experience in Northern Ireland, as well as on numerous reports from other high-risk locales, the author documents and compares the personal dangers facing fieldworkers across a wide band of investigatory domains. His purpose is not simply to catalogue the risks, but to offer some well-grounded advice as to what fieldworkers (and their advisors) can do to reduce such risks. In the end, risk will remain a part of the game if fieldworkers are not to shy away from potentially hazardous duty. But, as *Dangerous*

Fieldwork makes clear, courage in the face of danger is justifiable only when prudence is finely honed.

—John Van Maanen
Peter K. Manning
Marc L. Miller

ACKNOWLEDGMENTS

I would like to thank Nigel Fielding and Claire Renzetti for helpful comments on the first draft of this book. Robert Power was also kind enough to share with me his extensive knowledge of the problems involved in studying drug subcultures; and I am grateful, too, to Michael Fischer for conversations about the dangers involved in anthropological fieldwork. A number of people provided specific information about a variety of topics. I am indebted to Neal Grenley for advice about health and safety legislation in the United States, and to Patricia Mariani for information on the U.S. Occupational Safety and Health Act. I would like to thank Anne Corden, Patricia Ellis at the Institute of Social Research at the University of Michigan, and Cynthia Taeuber of the U.S. Bureau of the Census, all of whom provided information about safety guidelines in research organizations, and Jan Wathey of the Postgraduate Training Board of the Economic and Social Research Council, for information about the Board's current policy on safety issues. A final word of thanks goes to John Van Maanen for his helpful and constructive editorial support.

DANGEROUS FIELDWORK

RAYMOND M. LEE
Royal Holloway University of London

1. INTRODUCTION

The British sociologist Robert Moore (1971, p. 87) recounts how, during his research, the police told him to leave the site of a racially charged affray. "What does the eager researcher do when moved on?" he asks. "I ran around the block, took my coat off and strolled innocently into the middle of the battle again." Moore's comment nicely captures the indomitable character of field research in a way that many of its practitioners would recognize and applaud. Yet, the risks inherent in field research should not be discounted. Researchers often work in settings made dangerous by violent conflict, or in social situations where interpersonal violence and risk are commonplace. Indeed, in many cases it is the violence itself, or the social conditions and circumstances that produce it, that actively compel attention from the social scientist. To be sure, social research is safer, in absolute terms at least, than a not unrelated profession—journalism—similarly interested in violence and conflict (Sluka, 1990). The first 15 months of fighting in the former Yugoslavia, for example, brought the deaths of some 27 journalists and media technicians (Husarska, 1992); a rate of attrition, thankfully, not even approached by social scientists. On the other hand,

1

and this may be no more than an oddity, Howell (1990, pp. 11-12) found, using rather sketchy data, that rates of vehicle fatalities and deaths involving violence are appreciably higher for American anthropologists aged under 65 than for the U.S. male population, aged 30-64, as a whole.

As Jeffrey Sluka (1990) points out, the dangers researchers face in the field are rarely discussed in a systematic way. Instead, the matter has traditionally been treated lightly, as a source of "war stories" to be told informally, perhaps in a self-deprecating way, rather than as a methodological issue that needs to be addressed seriously. Howell, too, comments on the paucity of information available on the risks faced by researchers, or on how those risks might be managed:

> The library was searched for research directly on this topic, but it was found that to an astonishing extent the collections are silent on the problems of maintaining health and safety in anthropological fieldwork, and equally silent on the extent of the problems of failing to do so. (1990, p. 12)

In line with a growing awareness of health and safety issues in a number of disciplines and professions (Norris, 1990; Teeman, 1993; but see also Green, 1992), this lack of discussion is giving way to an increasing level of informed awareness about the hazards of fieldwork. Howell, who candidly records that her concern with health and safety issues was partly prompted by the death of one son and the serious injury of another in a truck accident while in the field, undertook a survey of fieldwork dangers based on a sample of American Anthropological Association members ($n = 236$). Using these data she tried to estimate the prevalence of a wide range of possible hazards, from war, robbery, and assault; through parasitic, infectious, and degenerative diseases; to mental difficulties, accidental injuries, animal bites, and hazards like frostbite and sunstroke that arise from exposure to the elements. In sociology, a number of writers have mentioned in passing some of the possible dangers that might confront researchers who work with deviant or stigmatized populations (Berk & Adams, 1970; Polsky, 1971; Yancey & Rainwater, 1970). More recently, those researching areas of violent political conflict are reporting on the difficulties they have faced (Peritore, 1990; Sluka, 1990), as have those conducting ethnographic research on drug abuse (Williams, Dunlap, Johnson, & Hamid, 1992). There has also been a growing awareness of the possible dangers faced by female researchers (Warren, 1988).

Beyond some discussion of accidents and disease, relatively little attention is paid in this volume to the environmental and biological hazards facing field researchers. As Howell (1990) points out in documenting a number of these hazards, a range of excellent general guides is now available for topics such as survival in hostile environments, coping with emergencies, and health risks. (For an annotated listing, see Howell, 1990, pp. 198-199. See also Ellen, 1984, pp. 206-208.) Nor is attention paid to the legal risks that researchers face from subpoenas of data or libel writs, or to the risk of stigmatization that sometimes attaches itself to those, for example, who carry out research on sexual deviance. (Discussions of both these topics can be found in Lee, 1993.) The emphasis instead is on hazards produced by human agency, particularly in situations of conflict, violence, and duress. In exploring the risks for researchers posed by violent conduct, one should of course avoid assuming a golden age, when fieldwork proceeded to its preordained conclusion in an atmosphere of peaceful tranquillity. For example, Howell (1990, p. 94) records instances, going back to the early years of the century, of anthropologists being killed by the people they studied (see also Noone, 1972). Yet it is difficult to avoid the conclusion that field researchers work in increasingly violent times. Major armed conflicts (using a fairly restrictive definition) had increased from around 3 a year following the Second World War to a figure in the upper 30s by 1990 (Kidron & Smith, 1991; Wilson & Wallensteen, 1988). The end of the Cold War brought a reduction in international tensions, but it was also followed by vicious ethnic and regional conflicts in the states of the former Soviet Union and in what was previously Yugoslavia. Violent conflict, exploitation, and repression remain endemic in some parts of Central and South America, the Middle East, Africa, and Southeast Asia, and Western countries have scarcely been immune to civil disorder, terrorism, and rising levels of violent crime.

It is possible to distinguish two kinds of danger that may arise during the research process: the *ambient* and the *situational*. (Similar distinctions have been proposed by Brewer, 1993; Sluka, 1990; Yancey & Rainwater, 1970.) Ambient danger arises when the researcher is exposed to otherwise avoidable dangers simply from having to be in a dangerous setting for the research to be carried out. A study of routine policing in Northern Ireland, for example, involved accompanying police officers in situations where they were potential targets for armed attack (Brewer, 1993). Situational danger arises when the researcher's presence or actions evoke aggression, hostility, or violence from those within the setting. For instance, urban ethnographers in some settings have been exposed to violence induced by the use of amphetamines or crack cocaine (Bourgois, 1989; Carey, 1972; Williams et al., 1992). Whatever form they take, the risks posed by fieldwork in dangerous settings have a number of consequences. They shape research agendas by deterring researchers from investigating particular topics or working in particular regions. The strategies researchers adopt to manage potential hazards, both to themselves and to those they study, are strongly implicated in the ethics and politics of field situations. Finally, awareness and understanding of the health and safety issues surrounding fieldwork have an impact on professional practice, particularly in relation to professional socialization.

This volume explores a range of contexts that pose risks to the physical well-being of fieldworkers. Within this framework are considered the nature of the risks fieldworkers face, how such risks are managed, and the wider methodological issues that they raise. First, in the remainder of this chapter there is an attempt to assess how far the presence of danger in the research process attracts or deters researchers from exposure to risk. Second, in an explicit departure from the main thrust of the book—the human hazards of research—the chapter goes on to a brief discussion of health issues, in particular some of the health hazards faced by anthropological researchers as well as the psychological costs of fieldwork in dangerous settings.

Chapter 2 looks at the hazards associated with research on violent social conflicts. It explores how researchers gain access to violent or repressive contexts, and how risks are frequently mediated by the degree of identification and/or sympathy the researcher has for one side or the other in the conflict. Accusations that the researcher is a spy occur frequently in field research. Chapter 2 examines how such accusations arise in violent social contexts and looks at their potential consequences. The chapter also explores the controversial issue of the relationship between ethnographic research and counterinsurgency.

In recent years a considerable volume of work on drug abuse has been fueled by concern about HIV infection. Researchers working in the area frequently point out that the hazards of researching drug abuse are often exaggerated. Nevertheless, drug researchers have found it necessary to be explicit about the risks they face as ethnographers and have produced much good advice on how potential hazards can be ameliorated. This work is reviewed in Chapter 3.

Chapter 4 also addresses some of the hazards involved in studying deviant groups, in this case those such as outlaw bikers or youth gangs. The risks of situational danger are high in studying such groups. The chapter records some of the experiences of researchers who have encountered violence or potential violence while studying gangs and outlaws.

Chapter 5 focuses on risks that arise for field researchers sharing the work lives of those employed in dangerous occupations. Taking up a theme from Chapter 2, Chapter 5 also explores a different kind of occupational hazard, the risk sometimes involved in studying workplace conflicts.

A number of accounts suggest that sexual harassment of and sexual assaults on female fieldworkers are not altogether uncommon. Chapter 6 attempts to shed more light on what has been until recently a relatively unexplored area.

Chapter 7 provides a brief reminder of the importance of eyewitness testimony to what we know about dark episodes in our history, such as the Holocaust. Using Bettelheim's incarceration in Dachau as an example, the chapter considers how research forced on individuals by involuntary incarceration can help maintain psychological health in the face of massive and deadly risk.

Chapter 8 suggests that social scientists need to develop strategies for reducing the risks they potentially face. The chapter offers some suggestions for developing greater safety awareness, a more active role in safety matters by funding and other agencies, and looks both at the development of safety policies in research organizations and at training for risk reduction.

The volume concludes by suggesting that field researchers need to approach potentially dangerous research with a stance of resolute awareness. By so doing they maintain the appropriate balance between the prudence necessary to avoid hazard, and the potential complacency inherent in a failure to take justifiable risks.

Danger and Willingness to Research

Researchers who enter difficult, dangerous, or unconventional research terrains are often accused by those who inhabit them of being thrill seekers (see, e.g., Polsky, 1971; Yancey & Rainwater, 1970). Although social scientists have generally dismissed such claims, it is legitimate to ask whether researchers have been drawn by the promise of excitement to potentially dangerous settings, or to taking unreasonable risks in carrying out their research. Responses to an item on Howell's (1990) questionnaire suggest neither widespread foolhardiness nor timidity. Relatively few people in the sample described themselves unequivocally as either a "careful and cautious person" compared with others or as someone who enjoys "taking some risks." The majority of respondents placed themselves firmly in the center of the continuum. One can also observe that social scientists do not appear to have sought out social settings that offer some of the more obvious opportunities to experience danger. Despite a burgeoning interest in the sociology of sport, comparatively little has been written, for example, about dangerous sports such as mountain climbing or parachuting. Those social scientists who have discussed such topics (Lyng, 1990; Mitchell, 1983) appear to have developed their interest in the sport before becoming involved in it as researchers. Finally, one can note that closeness to risky, momentous, or stirring events does not preclude detachment from them. As Thorne (1983) points out, academic researchers typically have involvements, commitments, and perspectives that prevent them from sharing fully the risks taken by those they study:

> [T]his is a recurring phenomenon: sociologists and anthropologists venturing into exciting, taboo, dangerous, perhaps enticing social circumstances; getting the flavor of participation, living out moments of high drama; but in some ultimate way having a cop-out, a built-in escape, a point of outside leverage that full participants lack. The sociologist can have an adventure, but usually takes it in a *controlled and managed* way. (p. 225, emphasis added)

Sluka has argued that, far from embracing dangerous situations, field researchers "select themselves out" of potentially hazardous research (1990, p. 124). Echoing Polsky's (1971) critique of the mainstream research tradition in criminology, Sluka charges that dangerous research has been avoided. That avoidance, he goes on to argue, is rationalized by exaggerating the difficulties involved in researching dangerous situations and buttressed by a neglect of strategies for coping with danger while in the field. There seems little doubt that the dangers inherent in some research settings have deterred researchers from entering them. Although, because of the possibility of question order effects, one should probably put too much weight on the specific figures, only a small proportion (3%) of the respondents in Howell's (1990) survey of anthropologists said they had been prevented from doing fieldwork at some time in their career because they judged the research to be too dangerous. However, a rather larger proportion (9%) recorded that fieldwork had not been possible due to political instability in a foreign country. In many of these cases it is likely that research access was denied by factors beyond the researchers' control, such as closed borders, visa restrictions, or disrupted travel arrangements; though it would be surprising if the risks inherent in an unstable political situation did not act, in at least some instances, as a deterrent to the research. According to Starn (1991), anthropological research in parts of Peru declined markedly following armed insurrection by Shining Path guerrillas. Graduate students who might formerly have carried out research in these areas apparently chose to work instead in Ecuador or Bolivia. In Northern Ireland, rural communities that tend to be relatively peaceful (for a review, see McFarlane, 1986) have been studied more often by ethnographers than conflict-ridden urban areas. (Urban ethnographies include those by Burton, 1978; Feldman, 1991; Jenkins, 1983.) Nor has it escaped notice that topics such as the operation of paramilitary groups, which are likely to pose risks to inquirers in Northern Ireland, have been investigated more readily by journalists than by social scientists (O'Dowd, 1986; though see Bruce, 1992).

Although it would be invidious to pinpoint individual cases, there are certainly instances where the reasons researchers give for not pursuing research in potentially dangerous circumstances read uncomfortably like rationalization. Yet, a disinclination to face risks is far from the only factor affecting the propensity to carry out dangerous research. The choices researchers make to study—or to avoid—particular topics are mediated by a variety of personal, aesthetic, theoretical, and ideological factors. For example, it is not uncommon for family, colleagues, and friends to express fears to a researcher contemplating research in a putatively dangerous setting. There is little evidence, however, that the entreaties of significant others have a substantial deterrent effect (Howell, 1990, p. 34). Even so, it may be difficult to calm such fears, because perceptions of the possible dangers involved are often shaped by sensationalized or dramatic media reporting (Sluka, 1990; Williams et al. 1992; Yancey & Rainwater, 1970). Matters of taste also steer researchers away from certain kinds of topic. Illegal drug use frequently takes place in locations that are dirty, dilapidated, and sometimes physically treacherous (McKeganey, 1990; Williams et al. 1992). Distaste or a lack of tolerance for such surroundings may deter researchers from seeking such locales as research sites.

Researchers sometimes shy away from studying violent social conflicts because they are uncomfortable with the modes of thought underpinning them. O'Dowd (1986) acknowledges that a considerable volume of research has been prompted by the "Troubles" in Northern Ireland. He argues, however, that research agendas have been shaped by assumptions that de-emphasize the centrality of the communal conflict. Clearly, partisans in the conflict find empirical research unwelcome because it potentially challenges their view that the conflict is immutable and intractable. At the same time, what O'Dowd calls the "cosmopolitan and Olympian view," frequently associated with liberal and academic opinion, assumes that conflict is abnormal and irrational and therefore seeks to avoid the empirical exploration of contentious issues. (Taylor, 1986, makes a rather similar point.)

Comparable assumptions are implicated, according to some writers, in the failure of anthropologists to predict the eruption of violent conflict in a number of erstwhile peaceful societies. Starn (1991) argues that insurrection by Shining Path guerrillas caught anthropologists unawares because scholars were committed to a view of Andean society as a timeless agrarian culture grounded in the preconquest past. In a similar vein, Dumont, commenting on Khmer Rouge violence, observes that, "History, with the might of its contingency, painfully shattered images of an all-smiling, easygoing people, gentle in their manners and smooth in their social interactions" (1992, p. 144). Starn's view, it must be said, is controversial (Mayer, 1991). Dumont, too, acknowledges that there may be limits to the parallels one can draw between Cambodia and his primary area of interest, the Philippines. Nevertheless, the point remains. A conceptual apparatus framed by exoticism or an overly narrow focus on traditional or symbolic spheres (Bourgois, 1990) may leave researchers ill-equipped to confront the realities of violence, conflict, or horror.

The political sympathies of researchers affect their willingness to enter settings made dangerous by violent political conflict. Radical critics of mainstream social science insist that social research has an advocacy role on behalf of those subordinated within structures of power, domination, and disadvantage. Such a position mandates and motivates ethnographers to enter and remain in repressive, violent, and coercive settings (Gilmore, 1991; Nordstom & Martin, 1992). Some writers maintain that the radical vision is a selective one. Protestant paramilitaries have been responsible for approximately half of the civilian casualties produced by the conflict in Northern Ireland. Yet, as Bruce (1992) points out, they remain little studied relative to scholarly work on the Irish Republican tradition. In his view academics and journalists, particularly on the Left, show greater sympathy and understanding for movements that can be interpreted as having an anti-imperialist role. They have little affinity for groups apparently lacking socially progressive aims and motivations. "Unloved groups," as Fielding (1982) calls them, are difficult to study. Being unable to identify with their aims and methods inhibits the kind of "appreciative" understanding (Matza, 1969) generally thought indispensable to the ethnographic method. In the absence of countervailing factors (Bruce, for example, is a distinguished academic chronicler of Protestant fundamentalism in Scotland, Northern Ireland, and the United States), such groups often also judge inquirers on the basis of their sympathies. Researchers may judge, rightly or wrongly, that a failure to pass muster in this regard might expose them to physical harm. Of course, what might be set in motion as a result is a self-fulfilling prophecy in which researchers do not seek entry to unloved groups, or settle for those with only peripheral involvement, because they assume rebuff. In the context of a deadly quarrel, though, an unwillingness to take the risk is perhaps understandable.

It is important not to assume research in dangerous settings is impossible (Lofland & Lofland, 1984, p. 17; Sluka, 1990). The risks inherent in researching dangerous social situations can be negotiated (Sluka, 1990; Yancey & Rainwater, 1970). They must, however, be approached with foresight and planning. As Sluka points out, dangers are never totally manageable and, as with anyone else, researchers can be unlucky. Like the gambler, though, the researcher needs to make a "concerted effort always to maximize skillful handling of the situation, while recognizing that skill alone is no guarantee of success" (Sluka, 1990, p. 124). In particular, it is important, Sluka argues, to evaluate explicitly the possibility of danger, its potential sources, and how it might be managed or exacerbated by the actions of the researcher. As Sluka points out, the possible risks can sometimes be exaggerated. As noted earlier, the perception that some social settings are dangerous frequently reflects media stereotypes (see also Williams et al., 1992;

Yancey & Rainwater, 1970). If they are not to be deflected or to operate in a foolhardy manner, researchers approaching such settings must seek detailed knowledge, particularly from people with firsthand experience of the situation. Sluka also suggests that, if possible, exploratory visits should be made to the setting, and the risks involved should be discussed with colleagues or supervisors. (On some of the difficulties produced by a lack of local knowledge, see Gilmore, 1991.)

Accidents, Illness, and Mental Distress

Concerns about the health of the researcher rarely surface in the sociological literature. There are some scattered references to the onset of physiological symptoms—diarrhea, nosebleeds, and vomiting—produced by the psychological stresses associated with fieldwork (Johnson, 1975; Punch, 1979; Walford, 1987). The issue of health risks to the researcher has been raised in relation to pseudopatient studies, where a researcher enters a medical setting in the guise of a patient in order to carry out covert observation. Bulmer (1982b), reviewing the ethics of pseudopatient studies, points to instances where pseudopatients suffered psychological and physiological symptoms, apparently resulting from the stress of maintaining the pseudopatient role. Bulmer also points to the possibility of unnecessary treatment being visited on the pseudopatient. Although he details no specific instances where harm of this kind has taken place, he alludes to a number of cases where successful maintenance of the deception required surgery prior to entering the setting.

Researchers studying drug use have confessed to fears about exposure to infectious diseases, although anxiety almost certainly far outstrips the possibility of infection in these cases. Despite medical reassurance that the risk was slight, Carey (1972, p. 82), for example, succumbed to a mild hypochondria in which every vague malaise was interpreted as the onset of hepatitis during fieldwork with amphetamine users in less than hygienic conditions. Although he recognizes that the risks are slight, McKeganey (1990), too, admits to anxiety about contact with infected needles. During an interview with a drug user who was HIV positive, the user took a needle, wrapped in paper, out of his pocket. McKeganey comments:

> I noticed that my anxiety level at this point peaked and I became uncomfortably aware of how confined a space I was interviewing him in. At this

point he dropped the needle to the floor and I think I must have involuntarily moved to pick it up because he said, "Don't do that. I'll pick it up" . . . I am certain that the reason he did this was in the knowledge that the needle may well have had the virus in it. I was both impressed at his reaction and shocked at my own. (1990, pp. 120-121)

In contrast to sociologists, anthropologists, in common with archaeologists, geographers, and the like, carry out fieldwork in areas that may be quite remote. Work in such areas can be dangerous. Anthropologists in Howell's (1990) sample who worked in areas distant from North America and Europe spent less time in aggregate in the field than those working in less remote locations, but reported exposure to a greater number of hazards. Where water or sanitation systems are not well developed, the risk of contracting infectious and parasitic diseases may be quite real. Transportation difficulties both increase the likelihood of accidents and may prevent timely medical intervention.

Although generally easy to prevent, accidents "account for most of the serious injuries and deaths that field workers experience" (Howell, 1990, p. 101). Cumulatively, 70% of the anthropologists Howell surveyed had to cope with an accident during fieldwork. Falls, according to Howell, are a relatively frequent occurrence during fieldwork and commonly contribute to deaths in the field. She draws particular attention, however, to vehicle accidents as a cause of death and injury among anthropologists. As Howell points out, the measures needed to reduce fatalities from vehicle accidents are well known. Death and serious injuries are lessened through the use of seatbelts, and helmets in the case of motorcyclists, and through the availability of prompt and effective medical care in an emergency. Anthropological fieldwork often involves traveling in remote areas over poor roads, in badly maintained vehicles, and where the use of seatbelts is not customary.

Howell identifies two diseases that frequently and seriously affect anthropologists: malaria and hepatitis. A common cause of sickness and death in many parts of the world, malaria is a parasitic disease transmitted through the bite of an infected female mosquito. In Howell's sample, substantial minorities of anthropologists (around one third or higher) whose fieldwork had taken place in regions outside Europe or North America had suffered from malaria. This highly debilitating disease produces recurring attacks of fever, sweating, and delirium. Malaria can be controlled by draining swamps and the like where mosquitoes breed, or through the use of insecticides, netting, or protective clothing to reduce the chances of being bitten. Regular small doses of antimalarial drugs also provide protection against the disease. However, not only should dosage begin before exposure and continue after it, but the schedule for taking medication needs to be adhered to rigidly. In a small number of people the drugs produce side effects, and in some regions drug-resistant strains of the malaria parasite have evolved. Because different types of the malaria parasite exist, different forms of the disease are found in different parts of the world. As Howell points out, doctors in Western countries often know little about malaria; therefore, the advice of a specialist may be needed about the drugs most appropriate to a particular region. In addition, some anthropologists, according to Howell, have reported delays in diagnosis and treatment of the disease because their physicians have been unfamiliar with the disease, which in some of its forms mimics the symptoms of other diseases.

Hepatitis A, according to Howell, "is very easy to contract, it can be found in practically all parts of the world, and it makes one terribly sick" (1990, p. 135). In all, one fourth of the anthropologists in Howell's sample had experienced hepatitis is one of its forms. (Type A predominates, although a sizable proportion of Howell's respondents were unable to specify what type they had had.) Experience of the disease was particularly prevalent among those working in the Indian subcontinent and in Africa. Howell notes, on the basis of further data from the survey, that preparing one's own food rather than relying on local cooks reduces exposure to hepatitis.

Howell points out that much of the information fieldworkers need about possible health risks in the field is available from published sources. Data on the causes of mortality in particular countries, which give a useful picture of health hazards, can be gleaned from the *UN Demographic Yearbook*. Bodies such as the Centers for Disease Control in Atlanta and the Medical Advisory Service for Travel Abroad at the London School of Hygiene and Tropical Medicine provide information about the prevalence of infectious and parasitic diseases in particular countries, specify inoculation requirements, and give advice about dealing with health hazards. (For bibliographic details, see Ellen, 1984, pp. 206-207; Howell, 1990, pp. 198-199.)

The risks to health faced by ethnographers are not just physical. There are indications that the stresses and strains of fieldwork have had ultimately tragic consequences for some researchers. Taylor (1986) alludes, for example, to a graduate student in Northern Ireland who "jumped off a bridge" after encountering fieldwork difficulties. Howell, too, mentions a number of unexplained deaths of researchers operating in difficult conditions that might have been suicide (1990, pp. 94-96). If there is a consolation in such cases, it is that they are rare. Howell (1990) examined more widely the extent to which the anthropologists in her sample reported symptoms of mental distress while in the field. Symptoms that might point to underlying mental illness, such as hallucinations or manic states, were reported only rarely by Howell's respondents. Rather more frequent were reports of depression and anxiety; 14% of the sample as a whole had experienced depressive episodes while in the field, and 16% reported anxiety states. As Howell points out, in some cases, where for example research is carried out in remote locations, the stresses of fieldwork are likely to be exacerbated by illness, nutritional deficiencies, and loneliness. On the other hand, fieldwork itself offers the researcher some protection against mental distress. First, ethnographic fieldwork presupposes active engagement in the field. Psychological research apparently suggests that, in the short term at least, those actively involved in coping with a stressful environment fare better in terms of mental health outcomes than those who are only peripherally involved (Heskin, 1980). Second, fieldwork is structured around "remissions" and "reminders" of various kinds. Periodic remissions (Schwartz, 1970) include spells away from the field; time-outs; retreats into fiction, solitude, leisure activities, and so on. Pollner and Emerson (1983) use the term *reminders* to refer to devices such as journals, "daily note taking, letters to and from the field, chairs of dissertation committees and the like" (p. 251), which allow researchers to avoid psychological engulfment by those in the setting. Clearly, remissions and reminders furnish ethnographers with a way of maintaining analytic distance on the field. They are also a means of maintaining psychological distance from the stress involved in fieldwork (Howell, 1990; Klatch, 1988).

On the negative side, strategies for maintaining psychological comfort provide opportunities for insulating oneself the field. Corsino (1987) found himself beset early in his fieldwork by feelings of awkwardness and discomfort upon interacting with people he did not know. As a result he withdrew at various points from data collection in favor of engaging in innocuous and nonthreatening tasks or interacting with people he found personally congenial. Although rarely reported, presumably because to do so might expose the researcher to disapproval from colleagues (Kleinman, 1991), this kind of underinvolvement in the research process is probably not uncommon (Wintrob, 1969). Even though many studies of dangerous situations show evidence of impressive researcher commitment, the temptation toward underinvolvement is likely to be strong in dangerous settings, given the stresses involved. "Better safe than sorry" is probably a useful motto in dangerous situations. However, the need for caution can also legitimate underinvolvement on the part of the researcher (Lee, 1992).

Hunt (1989) suggests that exposure to traumatic events in itself can cause researchers to omit or distort relevant data. She gives as an example an incident during her research on the police when she was confronted by a harrowing accident. Hunt records that her field notes relating to the incident contained a good deal of strikingly irrelevant information, and her estimate of the victims age was wildly inaccurate. A psychoanalytically oriented sociologist, Hunt sees such omissions and distortions as aspects of a range of defense mechanisms erected by researchers. These include physical responses, such as vomiting or a desire for sleep or food; through various forms of busywork; to feelings of depersonalization and/or amnesia. By invoking mechanisms of this kind, Hunt contends, researchers deal with the deep-seated wishes and fears surrounding images of illness, injury, and death.

2. RESEARCH ON VIOLENT SOCIAL CONFLICT

Violent or potentially violent situations are often highly sensitive in the eyes of those who control access to them. Although now rather dated in its details, the survey by Beals (1969) provides a catalogue of instances in which social scientists have been excluded from studying conflict situations. According to Beals, studies in border regions or areas of military significance are often restricted, as is research that takes place in the aftermath of war or revolution. Specific topics relating, for example, to the treatment of minority groups, to political mobilization, or to government popularity are also inadmissible in many countries. As Migdal (1979) stresses, however, it is important not to overestimate the barriers to research in such situations. He embarked on a lengthy attempt to obtain formal permission, from the military authorities on the occupied West Bank, to carry out his research in Arab villages, only to be told eventually that he needed no permission. On occasion, researchers have been able, with comparatively little difficulty, to gain access to relatively bounded communities where antagonisms are, for the most part, directed outward beyond the group. They have usually been able to do this by seeking endorsement from people of high status or good local reputation in order to give legitimacy to the research (Yancey & Rainwater, 1970). Thus, Migdal (1979) initially approached the village *mukhtars* (headmen) in order to gain access to the Arab villages he studied. Although their influence on local affairs was waning, the position and status they still had made it advisable to show them respect and secure their approval. Sluka (1990) gained entry to a Catholic enclave in Belfast with seemingly little difficulty. He initially contacted a local priest who verified his identity. Later he was able to move in with a martial arts instructor who was well known and well liked in the community. Association with this individual, who had in the past been imprisoned for politically motivated offenses and was widely trusted as a result, facilitated Sluka's acceptance by local people. In a similar way Burton (1978) seems to have been readily accepted in another Catholic enclave in the city because of his friendship with two students working on a summer project for local children.

A number of writers have found, somewhat to their surprise, that bona fide researchers are often welcome in factionalized and violent situations (Gilmore, 1991; Migdal, 1979; Wax, 1971). In some settings, researchers have been welcomed because of the security they provide for those being studied (Obbo, 1990). Bourgois (1990), for example, had some concerns about studying Salvadorean refugees in Honduras, fearing that the information he collected could in some way eventually be used against them by the authorities in El Salvador. He notes, however:

> In my exploratory visits to the refugee camps I was surprised to learn that the refugees desperately wanted foreigners to reside in the camps with them. They sought out my company because a foreign witness deters local military officials from engaging in random abuses. They assured me that far from placing them in danger, my physical presence granted them a measure of security. (p. 48)

More often those in the setting welcome the researcher as someone who can provide them with an audience and a voice. Indeed, in some conflict situations, the contending parties are sufficiently well organized to provide facilities such as political bureaus and press offices (Curtis, 1984). The staff of such facilities are often familiar with and helpful to outsiders such as journalists or researchers. As Gilmore's (1991) experience illustrates, receptivity to the presence of a fieldworker is often shaped by situational factors, as well as by a recognition that some opportunistic advantage might be gained from the research. Gilmore's (1991) request to study the Andalusian town of Fuenmayor at a time of political repression under the Franco regime was initially rejected. Apparently, members of the town's elite feared that he might be a political agitator. Gilmore comments, "The sudden appearance of an ethnographer in a factionalized community can fit into a proximate pattern of events and can be seen to be more than a coincidence" (p. 217). As he recounts, he had been unaware when he arrived in the town of a number of significant recent events. Some time previously, the eviction of a group of landless people from a large estate close to the town had generated negative publicity in the media. In addition, the local Communist leader, a charismatic figure, had recently returned to the town after a spell in prison, and there had been some increase in clandestine union activity. The decision not to grant Gilmore access to the town was unexpectedly overturned when he proffered—as an afterthought—a letter of introduction from a respected Spanish university figure of impeccably conservative reputation. This, together with the assumption that, as an American, he was anti-Communist, reassured a powerful and initially suspicious local official that he had no subversive intent. Gilmore goes on to speculate that the official at this point began to calculate that research from an apparently nonradical source might serve as a potentially useful counter to the bad press the town had received.

Access

Access to a research setting is never a given. What is open at one juncture can be closed at another time or in different circumstances. Brewer's (1993) proposal for a study of routine policing in Northern Ireland found favor with senior police officers because it was in tune with the value they placed on professionalism in the force. Following the appointment of a new chief constable, Brewer was refused permission for a further study. As he comments, "The chief constable who gave permission for the study has since retired, and the new chief constable seems to have a different agenda. The new management dislikes the idea that policemen and women are ordinary human beings who have not been brutalized by their paramilitary role; instead they like to think of the police as superhuman, extraordinary and unlike the rest of us" (p. 142). Access may also become more difficult the longer conflict persists. Although over time the presence of outsiders interested in the conflict can come to be taken for granted by local inhabitants, they can just as easily find the attention of researchers increasingly burdensome, as is apparently happening in some areas of Northern Ireland (Leonard, 1993). Deepening levels of rancor, generated as a conflict drags on, may encourage greater suspicion of outsiders. So too can increased exposure to surveillance tactics used by parties in the conflict. As part of her ethnographic study of a Northern Irish village, Bufwack (1975) tried to carry out a survey. Despite the villagers' otherwise friendly attitude toward her, the survey was met with suspicion and a high refusal rate. Bufwack attributes this to the army's use at that time of much-resented house-to-house censuses.

Researchers seeking to study violent social conflicts often face careful scrutiny of their background and intentions. Indeed, in many instances they are explicitly checked out by someone in the setting. The police may visit, seeking signs of subversive intent (Gilmore, 1991; Nash, 1979; Obbo, 1990), or run security checks designed to satisfy themselves about the researchers' probity (Brewer, 1993; Lockwood, 1982). Those outside the official security apparatus may also look for reassurance. In Northern Ireland paramilitary groups apparently satisfy themselves that researchers working in "their" areas have no involvement with the security forces (Jenkins, 1984; Lee, 1992; Sluka, 1990). Researchers also find themselves subjected to informal surveillance. During her work in Bolivia, Nash (1979) discovered that a neighbor, whose husband worked in the mine she studied, watched who came and went from her apartment, eventually reporting in Nash's favor that her visitors were rank-and-file workers. In some communities, children also function as a kind of trip wire against incursions from strangers. Leonard (1993) studied a working-class area of Belfast. Prior to her research she often walked, casually dressed, through the area without her presence being noticed. On beginning interviewing, she decided to dress formally by wearing a suit and carrying her papers in a folder. She recounts that, within a half hour, she was stoned by a group of children who took her "bureaucratic" dress to indicate that she was an outsider.

18

Researchers seeking through others to find a point of entry into a setting render themselves vulnerable to investigation. During his research in Mexico, Peritore encountered a journalist who promised to effect introductions to opposition candidates in the presidential election. While showing interest in the research, the journalist avoided being interviewed himself. Investigation revealed that he in fact worked for the political police. Peritore (1990) comments, "Had we gone with him, we most likely would have been delivered to a police 'safehouse' for extended interrogation" (p. 364). In another instance, in Northern Ireland, an initially helpful but subsequently elusive intermediary may in fact have been checking out the researcher on behalf of a paramilitary group (Lee, 1993). Seeking an intermediary can also expose the researcher to trickery. In at least one case a researcher has been approached by a potential intermediary who was apparently a hoaxer (Bruce, 1987).

In situations where the roots of conflict are deeply structural, the possibility of violence often restricts the methodological options open to the researcher. For example, as Sluka (1990), who carried out research in an inner-city area in Belfast, points out, being overeager to fish in murky waters can lead a researcher into trouble. So, although he asked his respondents about their support for the IRA, he remained careful to avoid subjects such as arms and explosives or the identity of members. Feldman (1991), who also carried out research in Belfast, puts the matter well by observing that "in order to know I had to become expert in demonstrating that there were things, places and people I did not want to know" (p. 12). In his study of oppositional politics in Latin America, Peritore found that Q-sorts, a methodology based on a card-sorting task, seemed less probing, and therefore less threatening, to respondents than depth interviewing. In a situation where many potential respondents had been tortured, this method had an additional benefit. It was rather less likely than an interview to remind respondents of an interrogation.

It is usually important in conflict situations to avoid any suggestion of a covert research role. Migdal (1979), for instance, carried out group interviews instead of interviewing respondents individually. The open and semipublic status of the group interviews quelled any suspicion that sensitive information of potential use to an enemy was being passed to the researcher. Both Migdal (1979) and Brewer (1993) found that openly taking notes allayed apprehension that information was being secretly recorded. Though covert research is to be avoided, one sometimes needs to restrict openness about the study to the research participants them-selves. Religiously intermarried couples in Northern Ireland, for exam-ple, fear intimidation; thus, they are wary about being identified as research subjects. In these circumstances, it is necessary to be selective about disclosing the topic of the research to a wider audience (Lee, 1992; see also Fountain, 1993).

Writers who have studied topics that are controversial rather than violently contentious have sometimes suggested open and simultaneous fieldwork with the parties involved (Bromley & Shupe, 1980; Spector, 1980). As Bromley and Shupe point out, such an approach has certain advantages. It allows the researcher to appeal to research participants' sense of fair play. It avoids the ethical and practical complications and potential feelings of betrayal that might arise from studying one or both groups covertly. Simultaneous study also produces what Gilmore (1991) calls "competition of communication." Each side strives to convince the researcher about the justice of its cause, increasing in the process the amount of data made available. This kind of approach becomes much more difficult where conflict is violent, in repressive contexts, or where groups have concerns about security. Here, maintaining a detached role can be a rather precarious business, requiring constant dissimulation, frequent realignments with one faction or another, and the ever-present threat of an unwelcome denouement (Gilmore, 1991). Indeed, in some situations concern about infiltration is so endemic that movement back and forth between contending parties becomes impossible (Thorne, 1983). In other cases the social topography of a divided society shapes the researcher's relationship to those being studied. Obbo (1990), who carried out fieldwork in Kampala during a time of economic unrest, refused lodgings in the house of one of the chiefs in the area she studied, a decision that earned her the trust of local people. The local official who allowed Gilmore (1991) to settle in Fuenmayor insisted on his renting a rather ostentatious house located in an upper-class area of the town. Dwelling in such a house would have inhibited Gilmore's rela-tions with working-class townspeople. To refuse it, however, risked alienating a powerful figure in the town. Gilmore and his wife managed the difficulty by stressing their inability as Americans to cope with anything other than sophisticated household appliances. Eventually, they were able to find a modest, neutrally located but suitably modern dwelling that simultaneously met their domestic, ethnographic, and political needs.

Feldman (1991) comments on the wider implications of residential segregation in conflict situations:

> As I became familiar with the topography of confessional communities [in Belfast], I realized that the only other people who were publicly moving back and forth in such a manner were the police and the army. I had to constrain the body as well as the voice. (p. 12)

Feldman takes this point further. In situations where those studied are subjected to detailed surveillance by social control agencies, "participant observation is at best an absurdity and at the least a form of complicity" (p. 12). Feldman's position seems overstated. Even in the repressive conditions of South Africa in the 1960s, van den Berghe (1967) managed in part to circumvent the many restrictions apartheid put in the way of his research; and writers like Burton (1978), Jenkins (1983), and Sluka (1990) have produced excellent ethnographic work in Northern Ireland under the kind of conditions Feldman describes. It might be argued that, far from being a form of complicity, refusing to carry out participant observation for the reasons Feldman suggests is in effect allowing the security forces to define the methods appropriate to social research.

Gatekeepers and Conflict

Research on organizations of conflict typically involves explicit negotiation with a gatekeeper. In these situations access may be difficult. In organizations like the military, for example, where a strongly embedded internal normative order provides a source of identity for its members, outsiders whose values are thought to be unsympathetic, or even just different, may be feared or greeted with suspicion (Spencer, 1973). Granting access carries with it certain risks from the gatekeeper's point of view. The research may expose unflattering or sensitive aspects of the situation, disrupt routine, or give voice to dissident elements. In addition, such risks have to be taken with relatively little information about the background or motives of the researcher and with nothing binding the researcher to protect the gatekeeper's interests. It is not unusual, therefore, for gatekeepers to allow the research to go ahead but only under restrictive conditions that allow them to monitor and control the researcher (Lee, 1993, pp. 123-133; see also Shapiro, 1987).

Both Gilmore (1991) and Nash (1979) faced attempts to control their work. In Gilmore's case the pressures were largely informal in character. Frequently reminded of the Andalusian proverb, "You are the people with whom you associate," he was exhorted to restrict his social circle to the town's elite and to avoid working-class or left-wing elements. By contrast, Nash, who studied Bolivian tin miners during a period of intense labor and political unrest, was told by managers at the mine she studied that interviews could only be carried out in an anteroom adjacent to a manager's office, and only after miners had finished their shift. Although Nash accepted this arrangement, she was fully aware that what was being said during interviews could be overheard and that the men were being required to give their time to her after completing a hard day's work. Only after some of the miners began to trust her enough to invite her to their homes was she able to escape the restrictive conditions imposed by the mining company.

There are situations, though, where social relations between those in subordinate and superordinate positions are structured in ways favorable to the researcher. Wood (1980) provides an example from industrial sociology. Wood argues that his access to a number of firms was facilitated by an institutional disregard for subordinates. In one of the firms he studied, industrial relations were characterized by an "indulgency pattern" (Gouldner, 1954), in which supervision of the workforce was minimal. Another firm, which also permitted him entry, was organized in a paternalistic way. In both cases, according to Wood, managers assumed that their workers would have no objection to being studied. In the indulgent firm, Wood was granted access and was left alone to carry on the research as he pleased. In the paternalistically organized firm, managers presumed to know what their workers were thinking. As a result, they granted Wood access in the expectation that all he needed to do was talk to a few workers to get a feel for what was going on. Similar situations may also occur in colonial or quasi-colonial situations, where gatekeepers assume initially that researchers share with them negative assumptions toward the local population (see, e.g., Diamond, 1964).

Researchers in this kind of situation typically seek ways to evade the gatekeeper's control. Often in doing so, however, they still face barriers. Association with those who hold power invokes distrust among lower-level participants. The police officers Brewer (1993) studied in Northern Ireland were by no means concerned only about the security implications of the research; they also worried that it might be used by management against their interests. The local bar culture made left-wing elements in Fuenmayor accessible to Gilmore. Initially, however, the town's working-class inhabitants were suspicious of him. He regularly went, carrying a briefcase, to the town hall to study its archives. Local people took this to mean that he was a lawyer, a negative attribution in a context where lawyers invariably served the interests of the powerful. Eventually Gilmore became accepted, but only after local Left leaders had carefully probed his political views and had decided, partly on the basis of his extensive and intricate knowledge of the prewar Spanish labor movement, that he was a progressive. Gilmore notes, however, that as he developed social ties with working-class and left-wing elements, his relations with the town's conservative elite became increasingly strained.

Ethnographers are often subjected by those they study to tests of various kinds. In some cases what is tested are the limits of the researcher's good humor and forbearance. In much of this there is probably an element of play. The researcher, like the apprentice or the greenhorn, provides a ready source of amusement. Accordingly, researchers are teased; given derogatory nicknames (Brewer, 1993); or placed in difficult, unpleasant, or compromising situations in order to see how they cope (Van Maanen, 1991). Tests may be rather more exacting in conflict situations. In some cases what is being tested are the limits of the researcher's tolerance. The migrant workers in the South African mineworkers' hostel studied by McNamara (1987) pointedly asked him to drink with them in the hostel beer hall in order to see how willing he was, as a white, to accept them as equals. Tests are also used to gauge the researcher's trustworthiness. Potentially damaging information is made available to see whether it finds its way into the wrong hands. Conceivably, tests of this kind are used to confirm the researcher's trustworthiness, rather than to diagnose it. Presumably such tests would not be used if those in the setting felt the risk of disclosure was too great. However, there may be some situations, as when the workers in the hostel McNamara studied forcefully voiced disapproval of their working and living conditions, where research participants feel they have relatively little to lose by their outspokeness.

Insiders and Outsiders

Researchers are commonly challenged about where their own sympathies lie in the conflict. Particularly when they come from outside the situation, researchers often respond to challenges about where they stand by proclaiming themselves to be neutral, explaining that they are present in the setting as an objective observer rather than an engaged participant (Gilmore, 1991; Sluka, 1990). Complete neutrality is probably impossible. It is unlikely that one's sympathies will be engaged to an equal degree by all the parties to the conflict. However, even claiming to be neutral may be more difficult in some kinds of situation than in others. Where social relations are highly conflictual, there may be no precedent or place for the neutral role (Gilmore, 1991). In many Latin American countries, politics are polarized around profound economic disparities, repressive regimes, and the actions of powerful neighbors. As a result, "assertions of scientific objectivity or neutrality can be perceived as being naive or as screening a hidden agenda" (Peritore, 1990, p. 360). Claiming neutrality can seem like an admission of spying, because in repressive societies the informer, by being noncommittal, leads others into indiscretion. Alternatively, the neutral researcher risks being seen as a "social eunuch" devoid of views and principles (Burton, 1978, p. 169), someone who plays both sides against the middle. So, instead of being universally trusted, the researcher ends up being suspected by all concerned. In other situations, the role of the neutral has some apparent legitimacy. Thus it seems that in Northern Ireland and in the Middle East, outsiders have sometimes been able to present themselves as neutrals because they stand outside local categorical distinctions and boundaries. Even here, though, acceptance of the researcher, at least in the first instance, may remain at a quite superficial level. In particular, as Bowman (1993, p. 457) points out, the researcher may be presented with a misleading picture of a group's internal politics, because in conflict situations members may be keen to display an impression of unity to the outsider, downplaying in the process internal discord, conflict, or factionalism.

Often when researchers proclaim their neutrality, they are in fact concealing their own sympathies. By doing so, they deceive at least some of those in the setting. A number of writers have argued that deception of this kind is permissible, indeed laudable, in highly stratified, repressive, or unequal contexts (Gilmore, 1991). Van den Berghe (1967, p. 185) records, for example, that he had few scruples about hiding his sympathies from the South African authorities in order to study apartheid. Wax (1971) quietly intervened to frustrate the ends of a violent faction in the Japanese relocation camp she studied during the Second World War. In addition, researchers radicalized by fieldwork in a conflict situation have abandoned neutrality as an appropriate ethical stance. Nash (1979), reflecting on the accusation that she was a CIA agent, became convinced that, "We can no longer retreat into the deceptive pose of neutrality" (p. 368). In the fears of her informants she recognized both the power exerted by the United States and the recognition that her own role was embedded within a colonial relationship between the United States and Latin America. From this realization, Nash took the position that it was necessary for social scientists to actively oppose U.S. government policy toward Third World countries.

On the other hand, as writers studying "unloved groups" have found, one may end up liking people whose politics one abhors (Fielding, 1982; Klatch, 1988). One may even come to understand how they reach the positions they hold, though still not agree with their views. Gilmore's (1991) account of his relationship with Don Miguel, the powerful local official who granted him access to Fuenmayor, reveals both annoyance and respect. Gilmore found tiresome his constant propagandizing for the Francoist cause but recognized that he had gained through Don Miguel some liking and respect for members of the town's elite, as well as some understanding of their concerns and fears.

For the indigenous researcher in a violent social conflict, opportunity, access, and security favor the study of one's own social group. To put this another way, the advantage researchers have, in being socially placed and accredited by preexisting links to the setting, also usually restricts them to studying "their own kind" (see, e.g., Jenkins, 1984). Indeed, researchers in this kind of situation often parade their insider status. Thus Leonard (1993), in her study of a conflict-ridden area of Belfast, initiated conversations about her own background. In this way, her informants could discover that she was, like them, a Catholic, and that she had grown up in an area not dissimilar to their own, both of which indicated that she could be trusted. Insider status can, however, be a mixed blessing. First, though insider status eases the researcher's passage, it does not provide a passport to unrestricted access. Despite being a Protestant studying a predominantly Protestant community in Northern Ireland, Jenkins (1984) found he was still limited in what he could observe. Female friendship groups, certain class categories, formal organizations, and the world of clandestine political and paramilitary activity all remained substantially closed to him. Second, insider status can also limit the researcher's ability to ask questions. The researcher who is a member of a particular culture may invite only incredulity by asking questions about it (Nakhleh, 1979). Moreover, as Nakhleh points out, particularly in conflict situations, trying to obtain multiple perspectives on particular events may put one's existing social relations at risk. Someone linked to the researcher who has provided information about an event may feel slighted if alternative accounts are sought elsewhere, because this implies that the first informant has provided an untrustworthy account. In addition, in some groups tacit limits surround the discussion of certain topics. Insider researchers can find themselves confronting what Mitchell (1991) calls the "paradox of intimacy." As he puts it:

Trusted intimates are expected to understand and assiduously avoid certain lines of inquiry. A breach of these expectations is particularly untoward when committed by intimates (novices may be permitted the occasional faux pas). Thus the paradox of intimacy: A high degree of trust achieved early in an investigation may actually curtail researchers' freedom to look and ask. (p. 103)

On the other hand, Leonard (1993) sometimes felt that her informants were too trusting. They often assumed that because she was one of them, they were doing her a personal favor by divulging sensitive information to her. Leonard was left, therefore, with nagging doubts about how far her research subjects could be said to have participated in the study on the basis of an adequately informed consent. This in turn produced an additional worry that research participants would feel betrayed when research results revealing potentially negative information about their area entered the public domain.

Leonard's (1993) informants helped her because in their eyes she was a "local girl who had done well" (p. 17). As this phrase implies, the researcher is often not so much an insider as a returner. He or she, although quite clearly a native, is often distanced from the setting by education and metropolitan ways sometimes acquired in another country. Researchers presumably often return to study their own culture because of the putative advantages offered by such a course of action. However, especially in situations of violent social conflict, the decision to go back and study one's own people may not be free of psychological significance. Jenkins (1984) notes, for example, that his decision to "take it all back home" rather than carrying out anthropological research on a historical topic, emerged partly out of a period of personal reevaluation following the death of a friend in a bomb explosion. Zulaika (1988), a Basque, returned as a graduate student to study his natal village at a time of violent conflict between the Spanish authorities and ETA, the Basque separatist organization. He records:

> I am still puzzled by something I did in my first months of field research. It is something I consciously knew was foolish, yet I seemed to have no control over the matter. Contrary to common sense and knowing that my professors would have been outraged, I asked for membership in the politico-military branch of ETA through a village friend who was a militant in the organization. I stated clearly that my only motive was to learn about the actual conditions of ETA activists life-style in order to write an ethnography about it. I had no willingness to give my life for the Basque cause, yet I was ready to assume all the consequences deriving from my membership in ETA. (p. xxvii)

The activists approached by Zulaika rejected his request. They felt that the presence of a researcher posed unacceptable risks to their security and enjoined him instead to study their enemies, the Spanish police. Zulaika's rejection by the ETA activists lends weight to the point made earlier that insider status does not of itself guarantee access to all aspects of the setting. Perhaps on the information available there is not much more one can say. Impulsive action by fieldworkers is not entirely rare. Bourgois (1990), for example, decided on the spur of the moment to make his dangerous and ill-fated excursion over the border into El Salvador. It may be significant that both this incident and Zulaika's attempt to join ETA took place soon after the researcher arrived in the field. Neither researcher was therefore encumbered by other involvements or claims on his time and may simply have responded to what seemed at the time to be a golden opportunity. On the other hand, it is tempting to suggest that the potentially dangerous course of joining ETA held a deeper meaning for Zulaika. The ETA activists are both outlaws and the purest embodiment of Basque national identity. Though stressing the impetuous and inexplicable character of his decision to join the movement, Zulaika also recognizes that it violates his supervisor's expectations. At the same time, he acknowledges elsewhere (p. xx) the guilt and anxiety he felt, during his adolescence in the late 1960s, at resisting involvement in Basque radical protest at a time when it had strong popular appeal. Conceivably, for Zulaika, attempting to join the movement was a symbolic act of transgression, overturning exile and reaffirming his identity as a Basque. In the end, Zulaika studied neither the ETA activists nor the Spanish police. Instead he explored a variety of Basque cultural forms, rituals, representations, and metaphors, transforming his ethnography into an extended meditation on the cultural roots of political violence.

Given the advantages the insider has in studying conflict, it is difficult to find instances in which researcher and researched interact *across* the significant social boundaries in a divided society. One instance where it is possible is in Brewer's study of the police in Northern Ireland (1991, 1993). Here an important contingency was the fact that his research officer, Kathleen Magee, was a Roman Catholic observing members of a mainly Protestant police force. The ability to negotiate a successful research role in these circumstances is affected both by the researcher's other salient social identities and by the availability of "exemptive typifications." The police initially defined Magee in terms of her gender (Brewer, 1993). For them, she was attractive, and her questions and interest in their activities served as a source of light relief from the boredom and rigors of their job. After a time, however, they became suspicious of her because of her religion. One night, news that a fellow officer had been killed began coming into the station where Magee was observing. As it did, one policeman launched a fierce verbal assault on her trustworthiness. As Brewer points out, because she handled the outburst well, the incident eventually aided Magee's acceptance by the police. It allowed them to define her as a "decent" Catholic; in other words, someone who did not support or condone political violence. (It also had the additional benefit of bringing to the surface issues about the purpose of the study and how the data from it might potentially be used in ways that made visible what those in the setting regarded as sensitive.) A final point to make is that, although the social environment was dangerous in this particular case, the research took place in a setting whose internal organization made it relatively secure for the researcher. Thus, in conflict situations, research across significant social boundaries may be rather more feasible in organizational contexts than in communal settings.

Personal Safety

For the researcher who operates in a violent social context, there are personal qualms about one's own safety to quiet (Van Maanen, 1988, p. 86). Burton (1978) has described the pressures of dealing with life in a city where bombs left in cars or in luggage were an everyday occurrence:

> In Belfast one generally walks around parked uninhabited cars with suspicion, casts unnerving glances at unattended parcels, scrambles to get home before it is too dark, maps out safe and dangerous routes for journeys, all in an effort to evaluate risks which previously could be ignored. (p. 20)

As Burton's description suggests, in situations of violent conflict the researcher, like others in the setting, becomes a "routine coward" (Lee, 1992); someone, in other words, who copes with ambient danger by developing a sensitivity to potentially hazardous situations and utilizing preventive strategies for avoiding them. The development of this kind of sensitivity is obviously important for the physical security of the researcher. The processes involved in acquiring knowledge and awareness of dangerous settings have further implications. Learning to cope in itself contains important clues to local culture. Shulamit Reinharz (1979) was involved in a study of an Israeli border town under bombardment from Palestinian fighters. She records the intense, continuous, and numbing fear that gripped her in the hours and days following her arrival in the town. Anxiety and overalertness impaired her ability to think clearly. For example, her preoccupation with danger made her inattentive to what other people were saying to her. She also experienced optical and aural illusions, hearing civil defense sirens even when they had not in fact sounded. Feelings of the kind Reinharz describes may not be unusual early in the field experience. Van Maanen (1988), for example, comments of his research on the police, "I can recall feeling as if I had a bull's eye painted on the side of my head the first few times I rode in the front seat of a patrol car" (p. 86). Generally, as time goes on, anxieties diminish. Reinharz began to develop protective strategies and rituals that helped her to cope with the fear and anxiety she was experiencing. Awareness of the strategies she adopted, and of the social contexts within which fear could be publicly expressed, helped lead her to an understanding of how others coped with the dangers facing them.

As a number of writers have pointed out, being able to use such strategies often depends on establishing a rapport with local informants and learning from them how best to deal with dangerous situations (Peritore, 1990; Sluka, 1990; Yancey & Rainwater, 1970). Having said this, researchers may still need to assess how far local judgment is to be trusted. It is clear from Reinharz's description that many of the "precautions" people took were of a magical character. Although they increased psychological security, it is an open question how far they increased physical security. One can also note, as does Sluka (1990), that local people sometimes disagree themselves about possible dangers. His informants, for example, were divided about how far his nationality would protect him in other potentially hostile areas of the city. Indeed, local people themselves may be no better placed than the researcher to predict the unexpected. Bourgois (1990) followed the urging of the refugees he studied and crossed the border from Honduras into El Salvador. Unfortunately, the Salvadorean army chose that moment to carry out a search-and-destroy mission in the border region. Bourgois was plunged into what he describes as a "fourteen-day nightmare" as he and the local populace, which included old people, women, children, and babies, were systematically bombarded, mortared, and strafed.

Simulation Methods

Some writers have suggested that social scientists should turn to simulation methods in situations that might be too dangerous to face in real life (Smith, 1975, p. 257). Research on social responses to disasters suggests that simulation may be useful in situations where danger arises from natural sources (see, e.g., Ekker, Gifford, Leik, & Leik, 1988, on the eruption of Mount St. Helens; Lee, 1993). One early use of simulation methods by an ethnographer is Agar's (1969) use of role-playing techniques with incarcerated heroin addicts. By this means, Agar was able to obtain data on events, such as drug busts, that might have been difficult to observe in situ. Simulations are not necessarily free from risk (for a discussion of the concept of risk in relation to simulation, see Crookall, Oxford, & Saunders, 1987). Two examples of situations in which the use of simulation or role-playing techniques had unfortunate consequences are the "Stanford prison experiment" and what became known as the "Stirling workshop." The Stanford experiment, which took place in the early 1970s, involved a group of volunteers who entered a simulated prison (Haney, Curtis, & Zimbardo, 1973; Zimbardo, 1973). Volunteers were randomly assigned to either the role of guard or the role of prisoner. After a short time violence and rebellion began to emerge among the prisoners. Some of them also began showing signs of emotional disturbance. The guards meanwhile attempted to harass, humiliate, and intimidate prisoners, and in some cases acted in a sadistic manner toward them. Scheduled to run for a maximum of 2 weeks, the study was terminated after 6 days. As Barnes (1979) put it: "the Stanford experiment shows that role-playing can become a collective *folie* in which people behave towards one another in ways that, under normal conditions, they would regard as reprehensible" (p. 131).

The Stirling workshop was an example of the "problem-solving workshops" that emerged in the 1960s as a new approach to the analysis of conflict processes (Hill, 1982). The participants were drawn from both sides of the sectarian divide in Northern Ireland. The workshop was held at the University of Stirling in Scotland, in 1972, and was instigated and led by Leonard Doob and William Foltz, two psychologists from Yale University (Doob & Foltz, 1973, 1974). As Hill (1982) points out, workshops of the Stirling type were designed to allow researchers to examine the dynamics of an ongoing conflict and to help participants in conflict situations learn, through the use of role play and related techniques, ways of resolving conflict in a peaceful way. Hill notes, however, that these attempts have not been altogether successful, partly because of the ethical difficulties involved.

The workshop was repudiated by academics who had been recruited locally in Northern Ireland to act as deputies at Stirling, and a lively debate about the aims, conduct, and outcome of the workshop followed (Alevy et al., 1974; Boehringer, Zeroulis, Bayley, & Boehringer, 1974). According to the deputies, "people living in violent social structures become involved in these exercises and thereby expose themselves to potential danger both intrinsic and extrinsic to the actual exercise" (Boehringer et al., 1974, p. 258). The intrinsic dangers arose, they argue, because the techniques used in the workshop were perceived by at least some participants as psychologically stressful. However, there had been no anticipation of this by participants. As a result, Boehinger et al. argue, there was no informed consent. The extrinsic dangers arose from the nature of the society from which the participants had come. In studying violent social conflict there are advantages to removing participants from the site of the conflict. Indeed, experiential approaches involving strategies like simulation and role play do not easily work in situ and need to be bounded in some way. Unfortunately, those who intervene from the outside in a social conflict can easily be suspected of being a *tertius gaudens*, the third party who benefits from the conflict of two others. Following adverse press publicity, there was widespread suspicion of the exercise in Northern Ireland, with charges that it may have been sponsored by the CIA. As a result, for many of the participants, according to Boehringer et al. (1974): "Stirling has become an embarrassment, something not to be associated with, something to explain away" (p. 272).

Ethnography and Espionage

Researchers are fairly frequently accused of spying. Indeed, one fourth of the social anthropologists in Howell's (1990) sample reported being accused in this way at some time during their fieldwork (p. 97). Glazer (1966) points out that strangers in conflict situations often become lightning rods, attracting to themselves otherwise latent feelings of hostility or suspicion; while Nash (1979), in a similar vein, suggests that allegations of spying may be akin in some societies to accusations of witchcraft. Dealing with unwarranted attributions can be stressful. For example, as Glazer (1966) points out, North American academics working in Latin America, and presumably in other countries, often have difficulty with expressions of anti-American sentiment. Expecting to be judged as individuals, they "experience a form of culture shock when ascriptive prejudice is directed against them" (p. 367). Nevertheless, accusations of spying may not be as immutable or as damaging as they at first appear. Indeed, they may repay careful study in their own right for what they reveal about the local community and the fieldworker's place within it. Murphy (1985) analyzed a series of rumors that circulated about him during his study of a working-class area of Seville. In sequence, Murphy was thought to be a CIA agent, a Basque terrorist in hiding, a secret policeman, and a refugee from an unspecified war. Finally (and jokingly), he was designated an alien from another planet and nicknamed the "Unidentified Flying Object." Murphy argues that the changing character of the rumors indexed his increasing acceptance by local people. Although the initial rumors all treated him as dangerous in one way or another, in sequence they placed him in an increasingly close relation to local people. Later, through the rumor that he was a refugee and the assigning of a nickname that stressed his strangeness, Murphy was symbolically located as being in the community but not of it.

According to Sluka (1990), suspicion is most common in areas of sociopolitical conflict, because governments, working on the principle of "know your enemy," use social science research to aid counterinsurgency efforts. As a consequence of this trend, Sluka contends, ethnographic research has become increasingly dangerous. Just as some criminologists (e.g., Polsky, 1971) regard the authorities as the major hazard to social scientists researching deviant behavior, Sluka and others see covert government action as a potential hazard for researchers working in areas of violent political conflict. Researchers have directly and knowingly aided intelligence services in a number of ways. In some cases, ethnographers have provided the contact and cultural knowledge necessary to attract and mobilize aboriginal peoples in wartime to act as scouts, trackers, or auxiliaries. For example, during the Second World War the anthropologist Pat Noone organized the Temiar people in the highlands of Malaya to resist the invading Japanese. Later, during the Malayan emergency, his brother Richard again organized them, this time in a campaign against Communist guerrillas (Noone, 1972). Richard Lee and Susan Hurlich (1982) record how, in the 1970s, the South African Army used a team of ethnologists to gather cultural data about ethnic groups in Namibia. The information gathered was used as the basis for a psychological warfare handbook designed to win the hearts and minds of local populations.

Academic researchers themselves have engaged in espionage. In a famous example, Franz Boas (1919) charged that during the First World War a number of anthropologists had abused their positions as scientists. They had introduced themselves to foreign governments as representatives of scientific institutions when they had in fact been spying for the U.S. government (Boas, 1919). (Hyatt, 1990, pp. 131-133, gives a detailed account of the affair. The letter is reprinted in Weaver, 1973.) The charges leveled by Boas received a hostile response, much of it underpinned by patriotic fervor and anti-Semitism. As a result Boas either was removed or withdrew from a variety of positions in professional organizations and associations. Ironically, in the light of its position a half century later, the American Anthropological Association dissociated itself from the views expressed by Boas and removed him from its governing council. By the 1960s and 1970s, however, anthropologists expressed particular concern about the activities of the U.S. Central Intelligence Agency in either recruiting or posing as academic researchers.

Attempts to gain access to data for intelligence purposes or to suborn researchers into supplying intelligence are less well documented than, say, attempts by law enforcement agencies to subpoena data. Nevertheless, Beals (1969), who headed an American Anthropological Association committee on Research Problems and Ethics that looked into the matter, wrote:

On the basis of circumstantial reports and personal "confessions," there is little doubt that a few social scientists have worked for the CIA or other intelligence agencies, while ostensibly carrying on research abroad. Almost certainly some CIA agents abroad have pretended to be social scientists. (p. 30)

Intelligence officers have tried on occasion to offer professional inducements to academics and others in exchange for information. Beals (1969, p. 139) mentions one instance of an offer by the CIA to provide an anthropologist with field expenses in return for furnishing political information. One can find, too, reasonably well-documented cases of intelligence sources in Northern Ireland seeking information from journalists in return for privileged access to fast-breaking news stories (Curtis, 1984, pp. 243-244). At a more transitory level, the CIA's Domestic Contact Division interviews travelers, including academics, about their contacts in and impressions of the countries they have visited (Johnson, 1989; Richelson, 1985). Beals (1969) comments, "Most questioning in my own experience and what I know of others' has been relatively naive and in some cases innocuous." However, he goes on, "in other cases questions have involved violation of privacy and the protection of informants" (p. 139). Following controversy over CIA activities on domestic campuses, relations between the Agency and academics became increasingly regulated and, at least on the face of things, circumscribed (Johnson, 1989). As Johnson points out, however, there remains considerable scope for academic involvement in research, consultancy, recruitment, covert activities, and direct intelligence gathering.

It is important, therefore, not to cast doubt on one's bona fides as a researcher. Beals (1969, p. 30) reports that at least one anthropologist may have been murdered because he was thought to be working for the CIA. Citing covert support for research by the CIA in the 1960s (see, e.g., Stephenson, 1978), Sluka (1990) suggests, for example, that researchers investigate the source of their funding in case it should raise doubts on the part of those studied. Unfortunately, even where one does take care to appear trustworthy, events can occur by chance or misadventure that potentially cast the researcher in a negative light. Suspicions have sometimes been aroused by unfortunate coincidences. For example, the home of someone Sluka (1990) interviewed in Belfast was by chance singled out shortly afterwards for a search by the army, inevitably raising questions about whether the two events were connected. In a similar but rather more tragic instance, a Mexican political activist was murdered the day after being interviewed by Peritore (1990). Researchers have also on occasion inadvertently disclosed potentially damaging information. Jenkins (1984), for example, left field notes containing sensitive material behind after an evening's drinking with some of those involved in his research. During a period of intense political and labor unrest in Bolivia, Nash (1979) lent her tape recorder, containing the unerased tape of a somewhat contentious interview, to a delegate at a union conference who subsequently played it back to his colleagues.

Mishaps

Of course, mishaps are common in field research. One psychoanalytically oriented commentator (Hunt, 1989) has traced the slips researchers make during fieldwork to unresolved intrapsychic conflicts of various kinds. More commonly, fieldworkers attribute such events to simple misfortune. Although this may be so, it is also pertinent to observe that episodes such as those described above arose from routine fieldwork practices. The researchers attempted to maintain good field relations through sociability and reciprocity or through being active and visible in the setting. These attempts backfired, partly because the stresses of working in a violent situation probably encourage researchers to make mistakes. Since those in violent social settings have a strong incentive to be apprehensive, mistakes or other kinds of untoward events do not go unnoticed. Moreover, it is likely that those disturbed by what has happened will try to discern if matters have resulted from someone's being involved as a pawn or player in a deceptive game. Goffman (1970) has analyzed in some detail the complex games of bluff and counterbluff that surround the covering and uncovering of spies. Researchers in each of the instances just cited were not drawn into such games. Aided, no doubt, by their own lack of sinister purpose, they were fairly readily able to dispel suspicion. Depending on the circumstances, they stressed to those concerned either the inadvertent character of what had happened, or else put on a determined show of carrying on as usual (both strategies again analyzed by Goffman, 1970). Nash assured union delegates that the incident with the tape was not a provocation but a mishap. In fact, she recounts that the episode actually diminished fears she was a CIA agent. The union delegates concluded that had she really been a spy, she would hardly have been so careless. Although shaken by what had happened, Peritore carried on with his research as normal, as did Sluka after only a brief pause. Each reasoned that to do otherwise, or to leave the setting, would imply guilt.

It is interesting to contrast these instances with Sluka's (1990) discussion of the nonfatal shooting of an American anthropologist by the IRA in the early 1970s. Sluka rejects the suggestion that the anthropologist was gathering intelligence. He points out, however, that the researcher's words and actions were scarcely reassuring. The anthropologist apparently spoke openly about having acted in an intelligence capacity during his time as a U.S. serviceman. He was in possession of British army intelligence maps of Belfast and had sought an explosives permit (apparently in connection with his hobby of underwater salvage diving). The researcher's work took him across territorial boundaries. As well as working in Catholic areas, he had carried out research on loyalist paramilitary groups and had associated with the leader of one of them. Uncertainty and ambiguity surround the events that led to the shooting. According to Sluka, the circumstances point more to a bungled interrogation than to an assassination attempt. However the incident was precipitated, it is not difficult to see how suspicions of an apparently sinister purpose could be aroused. An accumulation of apparently incriminating evidence becomes difficult to pass off as either incidental or accidental. Moreover, in conflictual settings association is often taken to indicate collaboration (Gilmore, 1991). As Sluka (1990) puts it, "it is not enough to be innocent, one must be *seen* to be so" (p. 117).

Research and Counterinsurgency

Ethnographic research carried out in a direct, open manner by a legitimate researcher probably has limited value as a source of timely operational intelligence for security agencies. Modern counterinsurgency techniques apparently rely on two complementary aspects of intelligence gathering. One of these is generalized surveillance. For example, the security forces in Northern Ireland engage in the routine and systematic collection of information about the population through tactics such as house searching, interrogation of arrestees, and the detailed tracking of vehicle movements (for details, see Hillyard, 1988). As a counterpoint to generalized surveillance, intelligence gathering also depends on the active targeting of suspects through the use of undercover operations and informants. The advantage of such methods to the authorities is that, in theory at least, they provide detailed and timely information, as well as possibly the opportunity to control events. (On the development, increasing use, and effectiveness of undercover policing strategies, see Marx, 1988. On "supergrasses" [highly placed police informers] in Northern Ireland, see Greer, 1988.) Undoubtedly, researchers collect data that could be of use to the authorities. The Northern Ireland example suggests, however, that security forces may be more interested in using general surveillance to gather quite specific information, such as details of car registration, or even the interior decor of suspect houses (Hillyard, 1988), of a kind that is quite peripheral to the concerns of most researchers. Again, at best, the researcher is likely not to be close to conspiratorial activities, which are probably more effectively penetrated by informers and agent-provocateurs. Marx points to the paradox that undercover activities of any magnitude often depend on a bureaucratic substructure that provides both funding and management support. In this context, ad hoc intelligence gathering may be seen as relatively ineffective. Furthermore, researchers may be more trouble than they are worth. They have reputational resources, are likely to have high status contacts outside the setting, and may not be so easy to discredit as others in the setting with a less ostensibly nonpolitical role.

None of this is meant to suggest that researchers should be complacent about the possibility of being used to gather information. Even if the foregoing analysis is correct, one cannot assume that the situation just described is duplicated in other contexts. Moreover, as Gary Marx (1988) has pointed out, undercover intelligence work sometimes relies on unwitting informants. Researchers may be used unwittingly without the fact, for obvious reasons, coming to light. As a result, therefore, researchers in dangerous situations need to proceed on the basis of a worst-case scenario (Peritore, 1990). For ethnographers this implies a data management regime organized so that information is held securely and rendered anonymous as close to the point of collection as possible. To minimize the amount of material that might fall into the wrong hands, Jenkins (1984) advises keeping field notes in a loose-leaf notebook. This allows notes accumulated during the day to be removed every evening and ensures that, at any given time, one is carrying around material relating only to the current day. Sluka (1990) suggests periodically taking or sending research materials out of the field (see also Nash, 1979) or keeping them in a safe-deposit box. The penalty here is that measures of this kind obviously undermine one of the strengths of the ethnographic method: a close and fluid relationship between the collection and analysis of data (Glaser & Strauss, 1967).

During the Vietnam war era academic researchers in the United States were widely involved as contractors and consultants in government-funded research projects on counterinsurgency. The rise and spectacular fall of Project Camelot (Horowitz, 1967) and the conflicts surrounding the so-called Thailand Controversy (Wakin, 1992) forced the ethical and political issues involved in such research out into the open. As Bourgois (1990) points out, the "at times polemical debates of the late 1960s and early 1970s have injected an important self-consciousness among U.S. anthropologists researching far from home" (p. 44). Researchers (not only, one might add, in the United States) became sensitized to the possibility that the information they had gathered might be put to nefarious use. For example, Faligot (1983) charges that community surveys carried out by social scientists in Northern Ireland "presented a formidable amount of data, which was simply added to the data banks of the Ministry of Defense, the Psychological Warfare Center, and the British Army Headquarters Intelligence section" (1983, p. 133). Faligot's claims are almost certainly wildly exaggerated (Taylor, 1986). Nevertheless, it is clear that "open source collection" of intelligence, involving among other things the systematic scanning of academic journals, is an important element in the gathering of intelligence information (Richelson, 1985, pp. 173-177).

Research Disutilization

Current ethical standards encourage researchers to minimize the potential usefulness of their research for intelligence purposes. Unlike evaluation researchers, say, who seek to maximize utilization of their research findings, researchers in areas of sociopolitical conflict may need to seek *disutilization*. Broadly speaking, the effective utilization of research depends on its visibility, its relevance, and its credibility (see, e.g., Rossi & Freeman, 1982, ch. 9). Visibility refers to where and how research findings are to be found, and research is relevant if it is timely and appropriate to matters in hand. Credibility depends on factors such as the reputation and competence of the researcher and on the methodological soundness of the research itself. Researchers seeking disutilization typically try to manipulate these aspects of the dissemination process in ways that make the take-up of their work less, rather than more, likely.

Disutilization strategies include outright self-censorship. In other words, potentially sensitive material is not published at all. Sjoberg and Nett (1968, p. 330) cite the case of the (unnamed) social scientist who would not publish his study of landholding in a Third World country while its right-wing government allied to the United States remained in power. Some researchers have chosen to publish in ways that are likely to minimize nonacademic interest in their work (Brewer, 1993, p. 141; see also Adler & Adler, 1993). Perhaps the most common strategy is to omit or garble specific details, to make identification of research participants or research sites more difficult. Jenkins (1984), for example, did not use "sensitive information"—implicitly about involvement in paramilitary activity—obtained during his research on working-class youths' lifestyles in Northern Ireland. A further possibility is to delay publication. Thus, Bourgois (1990) considered postponing publication of material he had collected in El Salvador:

> Although CIA analysts probably collect most theoretical studies on peasant politicization in Central America, I thought one manner of reducing the practical counterinsurgency value of such research would be delay publication—aside from periodic human rights reports—until the situation had changed sufficiently to limit the applicability of my data. (p. 49)

For a variety of reasons, not always having to do with fear of abuse, many of the strategies just described are relatively common in ethnographic writing (Adler & Adler, 1993). How effective they are in preventing the misuse of research information is open to question. Nor are they without their difficulties. First, and fairly obviously, not publishing, or publishing only in out-of-the-way places, can have negative career consequences. Second, as Bourgois comments, it hardly seems appropriate to allow intelligence agencies to shape the terms of academic debate. At the same time, as Barnes (1979) commenting on the use by U.S. Special Forces of ethnographic writing on the Vietnam Highlands points out, it will often require an unusual degree of prescience to recognize the future negative potential of what is for the moment apparently innocuous material. Finally, "[T]he community of scholars loses when we are duped, deceived or misled by the transformation or omission of relevant data" (Adler & Adler, 1993, p. 262). Self-censorship produces a biased universe of research findings and little chance of assessing either the direction or extent of such bias. It also inhibits methodological openness. It is noticeable, for instance, that few details of the research procedures used appear in Bruce's (1992) book on Protestant paramilitaries in Northern Ireland. (Gambetta, 1993, is reticent in a similar way about his research on the Sicilian mafia.) Though reticence is understandable, given the difficult circumstances under which the research was carried out, the excision of methodological detail seems excessive. Presumably some discussion of the problems and issues involved is possible without compromising either the identity of research participants or the security of the researcher. The absence of methodological detail potentially hampers further work in the area and may reinforce the tendency for researchers to shy away from dangerous topics.

3. DRUG-RELATED VIOLENCE

Operating in the world of illegal drug use brings with it a range of potential dangers. Bourgois (1989) found a "culture of terror" surrounding crack cocaine dealing in New York. The structural incentive to deal drugs is high, given both the financial reward they bring and the lack of alternative economic opportunities in inner-city areas. Dealers use violence routinely to maintain their credibility and status and to protect themselves from being ripped off. Random drive-by shootings have been a feature of some locales where drugs are widely used. Although, as Williams et al. (1992) point out, the media exaggerate the frequency of their occurrence, in such areas exposure to stray gunfire is a possibility. Amphetamines and crack can induce feelings of irritability or paranoia in users. These may engender disputes or fights and can be translated into physical aggression or attack directed at the fieldworker

(Carey, 1972; Williams et al., 1992). Patricia Adler (1985) and her husband established long-term relationships with a number of upper-level drug dealers in Southern California. She notes that sustained drug use made informants behave erratically, moving back and forth between trust and suspicion. Adler speaks of a number of (unspecified) threats from informants regarding the collection of taped interviews with drug dealers that she and her husband had built up over the course of the research. Such threats eventually led them to pass the tapes secretly to a third party uninvolved in the research for safekeeping. A good deal of illegal drug use takes place in run-down or abandoned inner-city tenement buildings (McKeganey, 1990; Williams et al., 1992). Such buildings are often structurally unsafe, with defective stairways and treacherous floors. They may even on occasion be booby-trapped to deter entry by the police or by thieves. In some settings researchers are in danger of robbery or of being pestered, sometimes in a threatening manner, for money (Berk & Adams, 1970).

Drawing on their experience over a number of years in narcotics research, Williams and his colleagues (1992) have recently reviewed a range of issues relating to personal security when researchers undertake work in the drug subculture. Williams et al. point out that although hazards do exist, the possibility of danger can be overstated. In part, perceptions of the dangers involved are fueled by media interest in the more violent aspects of the drug subculture and stereotypical conceptions of inner-city areas. Over the years, for example, they have encountered only a few examples of physical violence directed toward ethnographers (for a similar point, see also Johnson et al., 1985). Nevertheless, Williams et al. emphasize that potential dangers should not be taken lightly. Research is possible in such contexts but requires for its successful execution reliance on the arts of prescience, evasion, interpersonal management, and timely exit.

Personal style and demeanor are important in the kinds of potentially dangerous situation discussed here. Researchers, for example, should not dress or act in ways that elicit undue attention (Berk & Adams, 1970). Yancey and Rainwater (1970) record that a researcher on their project tried to facilitate access by rather freely buying drinks for potential informants in bars. As they recount, "After he had done this twice, the bartender approached one of the other members of the research staff and said, 'Tell that guy to stop buying drinks for everybody and leaving his money on the bar or he'll end up with a cap [bullet] in his ass' " (p. 264). Adopting a self-confident and determined demeanor can also be important. To do otherwise by appearing fearful or irresolute can denote potential victim status to those in the setting (Williams et al., 1992). Bourgois (1989) notes, for example, that his refusal to retaliate after an incident in which he was robbed caused some of those around him to doubt his self-respect.

The aims of a research study often impose conditions on who is eligible to be included in the research. At the same time, researchers may find it appropriate, for operational or ethical reasons, to offer some inducement in the form of money or services to participate. In impoverished settings such inducements often invite the attentions of ineligible respondents who seek to be recruited to the project (Biernacki & Waldorf, 1981). It is not unknown for such individuals to react in an angry or threatening way when they are turned down for inclusion in the project (Johnson et al., 1985). Although the actual level of danger to the researcher is probably not great in these instances, strategies for "cooling out" ineligibles may have to be devised.

Those who deal drugs seek to maintain their social invisibility by avoiding disclosure of their identities, whereabouts, and activities. As Williams et al. point out, approaching such individuals directly is highly threatening because it implies that the attempt to maintain invisibility has been unsuccessful. In these circumstances dealers may be tempted to identify the researcher as an informer or undercover agent and retaliate accordingly. Williams et al. point to a number of ways in which this possibility can be obviated. For example, various strategies to establish credentials can be used to differentiate the researcher from the undercover police officer or someone with hostile intent. Williams for example, shows potential informants a book he has written as a way of establishing his bona fides (Williams et al., 1992, p. 349). In the United States, a number of federal statutes authorize researchers to maintain the privacy of research subjects and protect data from forced disclosure to a court or administrative hearing (Knerr, 1982). In general, it seems that grants of confidentiality have allowed research to be undertaken that might otherwise not have been. The ability to show potential informants a Certificate of Confidentiality also apparently increases levels of cooperation from those, such as drug dealers, who are at risk if their activities are disclosed (Nelson & Hedrick, 1983). Williams et al. point, though, to one particular drawback in using this strategy. A key informant interviewed by Williams took the word *federal* on a Certificate of Confidentiality to mean that the researcher was working "with the Feds." As they comment, "the term 'federal' had a very different and unfavorable referent for dealers" (1992, p. 371).

Sponsors

Anderson and Calhoun (1992) point out that certain groups on the street—in the case of their research, the homeless and male prostitutes—have little ability to insulate their activities. As a result they can be approached by researchers directly without the need for intermediaries. Access to other groups, however, may be extremely difficult without aid from someone within the setting. Indeed, the importance of being socially sponsored by someone well known and trusted in the setting is a recurrent theme in the literature on access in ethnographic research. Exemplary sponsors like "Doc" and "Tally" are celebrated figures. Sponsors facilitate acceptance of the researcher. To introduce a stranger into a new social world, especially a deviant one, helps to guarantee the stranger's trustworthiness. In a similar way, a sponsor can help the researcher gain acceptance and allay suspicion by giving advice on how to avoid naive or overinquisitive questions or inappropriate ways of acting. Acquiring a sponsor is often treated in the fieldwork literature as a matter of good fortune. In fact, the availability and usefulness of sponsors are frequently structural matters that depend on factors such as the size, density, and character of social networks (Lee, 1993). There seems to have been a trend in studies among drug abusers for the role of sponsor to be institutionalized and, to an extent, professionalized. Former users and dealers increasingly operate on a paraprofessional basis, performing the dual paid role of locating potential informants and vouching for the researcher (Johnson et al., 1985; Power, 1993; Williams et al., 1992). In many cases, such workers have local reputations as former participants on the drug scene, sometimes with convictions for drug-related offenses:

> Prison is also an important place where dealers have met persons whom they can trust as "safe." One dealer commented, "Serving time tells what a man is made of." The norms among prisoners and ex-prisoners eliminate the chance that the individual is an informant or an undercover cop. (Williams et al., 1992, p. 353)

Using such individuals in a paraprofessional research role is not without its difficulties (Walker & Lidz, 1977). Staff turnover can be high. For some, the pull of the street is too strong. Doubt or cynicism about the efficacy of research has sometimes produced antagonistic relations between project paraprofessionals and more affluent, highly educated, and academically committed research staff (Broadhead & Fox, 1990; Fox, 1991). Street-based workers are sometimes constrained in their ability to log data. Chosen, after all, for their social proficiency on the street, some have limited linguistic and literary skills (Johnson et al., 1985; Walker & Lidz, 1977). Finally, as Roth (1966) pointed out long ago, in social research no less than in other occupational contexts, "hired hands" engage in output restriction and deviate from mandated procedures (see also Power, 1993).

In addition, however, in potentially dangerous settings sponsors also operate in a protective capacity. They can warn the researcher of imminent danger or draw attention to the ethnographer's presence in volatile or threatening situations. McKeganey (1990) recounts, for example, an instance when people inside the setting he was observing went out to a car that drew up outside. When he joked that he should go out and do some interviews, he was told that was inadvisable and warned that he was observing too much. Concluding that "some kind of major drug transaction" had occurred, he observes that "it would have been very unwise, and potentially dangerous, to have attempted any-thing more than a very detached observational monitoring of these events" (p. 119).

According to Williams et al., the role of protector also often emerges spontaneously. Provided they have no reason to doubt the identity or integrity of the researcher, individuals in the setting may give them-selves the responsibility of protecting the researcher by acting, for example, as a guide through derelict buildings. More generally, in the settings Williams et al. studied, there existed a general normative injunction to "watch backs." Operating in relatively hazardous settings, people felt obligated to warn each other of impending danger. Paradoxi-cally, protection in these circumstances can sometimes take hostile forms. Williams et al.(1992) note that threats, pushes, and slaps directed at the fieldworker can actually constitute "respect for the ethnographer" (p. 370). Often a direct signal that the researcher would be wise to leave the setting, they should be complied with immediately. Against this, one can also note that associations with particular individuals, far from providing protection, sometimes invite danger. Bourgois (1989) found his relations with others could have unfortunate consequences. In contrast to Williams et al., who stress the underlying stability of crack house organization, Bourgois emphasizes the social value of ruthlessness in the crack economy. The ability of dealers to deploy violence in a ruthless way ensured compliance from others and enhanced their social status. In this situation, Bourgois's associating with someone noted for relative timidity encouraged others to violence, safe in the knowledge they would not face retaliation.

Safety Zones

Research in dangerous situations depends on the maintenance of safety zones that allow researcher and researched to operate in a secure manner (Williams et al., 1992). What Williams et al. seem to suggest is that the researcher should feel able to remain within the setting, provided a set of environmental and social conditions are met. The safety zone encompasses a physical area that extends for a short distance around the fieldworker. Within this area the researcher should feel physically secure and psychologically at ease, free from environmental hazard or interpersonal danger. The safety zone also permits others in the setting to feel that the researcher is not intruding upon them or presenting a threat to their security. Establishment of a safety zone depends in part on the social acceptance of the researcher by those within the setting. It also depends, however, on the researcher's carefully, even subliminally, sizing up the setting and entering and remaining in it only if it seems that the safety zone can be maintained.

Drawing on animal ethology and dramaturgical theory, Goffman (1971) explored how individuals maintain feelings of physical security in potentially threatening environments. Human beings, according to Goffman, pervasively, though usually peripherally, scan their physical and social environment for indicators of threat. Within settings four elements exist "along which the signs and sources of alarm are distributed and articulated" (1971, p. 329). First, security and threat are both constrained within a "furnished frame," a built environment with specific design and structural features. Second, within settings a variety of spaces exist that fall beyond an individual's line of sight and that might hide potential hazards. Such areas—"behind one's back," behind partitions, and areas of darkness—Goffman refers to as "lurk lines." Third, settings also have "access points"; spaces for entry and exit on the thresholds of which individuals may be vulnerable. Finally, Goffman notes that the individual's "social net," by which he means those co-present in the setting, provide through expressive gestures information concerning levels of threat present in the environment. Presumably, the appearance of each of the elements Goffman describes helps field-workers to determine the location of safety zones. In addition, according to Williams et al., ethnographers working in the kinds of settings they describe rapidly develop a sixth sense about potential dangers. This presumably comes about as they learn to detect even sometimes subtle perturbances associated with the furnished frame, the lurk lines, and the access points in the setting and the activities of others immediately present.

Tense situations easily arise in drug-related settings. Fights, disputes, and confrontations can break out, even over apparently trivial matters (Power, 1989). Williams et al. suggest that when trouble of this kind looms, the researcher is well advised to avoid it or to leave the setting altogether. Although in doing so one loses data, information about violent episodes can still be obtained, using interviews rather than direct observation (Carey, 1972). Though drug locales exhibit high levels of mistrust, paranoia, and potential violence, they are also socially organized to control disruption due to these causes (Williams et al., 1992). In some cases, the presence of an outsider in the person of an ethnographer can itself help to minimize violence. Moreover, when confrontation flares, researchers have a number of advantages that may allow them, if required, to deal with the situation in a controlled way. They are not under the influence of drugs (but see Adler, 1985, p. 24). Nor are they themselves parties to disputes that may arise. Their understanding as social scientists of the interpersonal dynamics of social situations also provides them with a set of resources for dealing with tense situations. Particularly important in this regard, Williams et al. suggest, is the use of humor and the fieldworker's neutral stance toward disputes. It can be possible to defuse tense situations, for example, by telling funny stories or through the researcher acting as mediator. Carey (1972) makes a similar point. The drug-induced state that produces aggression by amphetamine users also makes them easy to distract. Users in Carey's study could therefore often be diverted from their aggressive actions.

Inciardi (1993) observes that researchers inevitably encounter in crack houses those trapped by drug use into a downward spiral of degradation. In such situations, which can be harrowing to observe, the impulse to help can be strong. Inciardi makes the point, however, that a researcher's ability to intervene directly can be quite strictly limited. He records, for example, being threatened with death if he intervened in the sexual abuse of a teenage girl by a group of men. Instead, he maintains "there are many other things that can be done—later, subtly, and however temporarily" (1993, p. 155). In his case this included giving advice to crack users about treatment programs or, in one instance, providing routine hygiene to a neglected baby.

Where drug dealers compete, violent means in the form of armed robbery, drive-by shootings, and firebombings may be used to increase market share, maintain a competitive edge, or enforce territorial boundaries (Bourgois, 1989; Williams et al., 1992). Such situations are obviously dangerous for those who may become caught up in them. However, Williams et al. suggest that a number of factors serve to minimize the exposure of researchers to such hazards. Despite some tendency for the media to describe them as haphazard occurrences, such activities are usually quite specifically targeted on rivals, and in many cases take place out of sight. Ethnographers, moreover, may have some warning of tensions or disputes and can possibly avoid the more obviously dangerous settings. Sometimes, of course, this will not be possible. As Williams et al. (1992) comment, "These are not situations for mediation or humor, only for getting out of the way or following orders" (p. 366).

Williams et al. note that in the settings they studied, researchers were often asked for money in an importuning, and sometimes threatening, way. Although as a matter of general policy they pay research subjects in order to reciprocate for their cooperation, they found it necessary to develop a variety of strategies "to minimize criminal victimization and monetary losses" (1992, p. 365). One can take care, for example, to carry only relatively small amounts of money or to conceal it, perhaps by distributing it among different pockets or hiding some in a shoe. It may also be appropriate to develop an expectation that one will contribute to the setting but in a generalized way, for example, by sharing in the purchase of drinks, food, and cigarettes.

Relations With the Police

Ethnographers studying drug scenes have generally been cautious in their dealings with the police. In so doing they avoid drawing the people they study to official attention. They also forestall the possibility that talking to the police will be misconstrued as the passing on of information. Indeed, the quality of a researcher's relations with the police may be taken by local people as an indication of trustworthiness. Bourgois (1989) notes, for example, that being roughly questioned on one occasion by a police officer enhanced his legitimacy in the eyes of those around him (see also Anderson & Calhoun, 1992; Leonard, 1993). Conversely, the ethnographer also provides a measure of protection to those in the setting. Williams et al. record several instances where the presence of a researcher apparently deterred police officers from ill-treating suspects.

In a few cases ethnographers have been arrested. For example, Inciardi (1993) entered the front of a crack house in Miami while police were in the process of breaking in at the rear. Everyone in the house, including Inciardi, was arrested. He then spent several hours in jail while those taken in the swoop were processed. Because he was not in posession of drugs or a weapon, and had identification that indicated his status as a researcher, Inciardi was released. Williams et al. (1992) observe that arrests of this kind are rare, an observation borne out more widely by Howell's data (1990, p. 96). Only 5% of her sample of anthropologists reported having been arrested while carrying out fieldwork, with arrests occurring less commonly in North America and Europe than in other parts of the world. (Howell gives little information about the circumstances leading to arrests or their outcome, presumably because her data are based on anonymous self-reports. She does indicate, though, that in at least some cases, serious charges were involved. In one instance the leader of a research team was charged with murder, and in two cases researchers in Latin America were charged with drug smuggling.)

In the event of being detained by the police, Williams et al. recommend that researchers allow themselves to be arrested and taken into custody. They should, however, produce identification during booking procedures, arrange for legal representation, and attempt to have charges dropped. (Apparently, some research teams working on drug-related projects now retain a lawyer to ensure speedy resolution of legal problems.) Arrest can pose particular problems for covert researchers. Identifying oneself as a researcher may prevent charges from being brought, but at the cost of revealing the nature of the study to the police and to other arrestees. Humphreys (1970) was arrested near a tearoom during the course of his research on impersonal sex in public restrooms (pp. 94-96). Stephen Small (1983) was arrested at a demonstration while carrying out a covert participant observation study of a group of young black people, as part of a large-scale, multimethod study of police-public relations in London (pp. 148-154). Neither Humpheys nor Small disclosed his identity as a researcher to the police during the arrest or subsequent booking. Small, who is black, was treated abusively by the police and was threatened with being held for 7 days when he refused to give his fingerprints. His next of kin were given false information, possibly in error, about his whereabouts. Humphreys records that with the help of "an astute attorney" the charge of loitering brought against him never came to court. Small's case proceeded to trial. Just prior to that, he and the director of the research project indicated to senior police officers at Scotland Yard that they would introduce evidence at the trial about his status as a researcher. Although the case went ahead, the arresting officer, in somewhat mysterious and convenient circumstances, proved unable to attend the trial and the case was dropped.

A further hazard of arrest is that it can bring the research to the attention of the police. Armstrong (1993) studied soccer fans in a Northern English town. He was arrested along with a group of other fans following an incident in which a rival fan was injured. Although Armstrong and the others arrested with him were released without charge, he records that a number of police officers subsequently indicated to him in a somewhat threatening manner that they knew who he was and what he was doing. Meanwhile, ironically, the fans he was studying suspected him of being a police spy.

4. GANGS AND OUTLAWS

The phrase *gangs and outlaws* is a rather loose and catchall designation. It refers to groups with varying levels of organizational sophistication, frequently at odds with the wider society, who use violence for the purposes of internal discipline and/or external aggression. Groups of this kind range from a dozen adolescents defending their turf against rival gangs, through chapters of groups such as the Hell's Angels, to armed and politically extreme survivalist groups (Mitchell, 1991) or the Sicilian *mafiosi* studied by Gambetta (1993). There are barriers to studying such groups for academics, especially those who are middle-aged, middle-class, and conventional in outlook. Some groups, like survivalists, are secretive. Others, outlaw bikers for instance, maintain strict boundaries between themselves and nonmembers (Wolf, 1991). Fearing infiltration by undercover police, they are recurrently suspicious and distrustful of outsiders (Hopper & Moore, 1990). They are also resistant to standardized research instruments, such as questionnaires or formal interviews.

Mitchell (1991) notes that some groups intentionally dramatize the contrasts between their own practices and those of outsiders. In taking these self-presentations at face value, outsiders are in some danger of producing superficial or exaggerated accounts. The ethnographer's ability to produce portraits of such groups from the inside is therefore important. However, the risk of the ethnographer's incurring violence in the process, though by no means loudly voiced, is a recurring motif in accounts of research on gangs and outlaws. Because of these groups' sensitivity to outsiders and the potential dangers involved, researchers have either relied on opportunistic access to such groups or studied them by covert or semicovert means. In the case of Hopper and Moore (1990), who studied women in outlaw motorcycle gangs, Moore's status as the former president of an outlaw biker club facilitated their access to a number of bikers' groups. While Wolf did not conduct a covert study, he rode with the bikers he eventually studied for an extended period before seeking permission to carry out his research. Where entry based on insider involvement is unavailable, researchers not infrequently present themselves as either potential members or sympathizers. Attempting entry in this way is often premised on what Mitchell (1991) calls "faith in transparent disguise" (p. 105); in actuality, researchers, in presenting themselves as available for membership, often inadvertently emphasize the differences between them and those they study. Attending a paramilitary exercise conducted by survivalists, Mitchell tried to select clothes and equipment appropriate to the occasion. However, his middle-class notions of outdoor accouterment proved ludicrously and noticeably different to those around him. As Mitchell observes, what saves this kind of situation from disaster is that, as in his case, the artlessness of the novice is often mistaken for enthusiasm.

Not everyone can be counted upon to be so charitable, however, and disguises can be transparent in more ways than one. Wolf's (1991) attempt to gain access to an outlaw biker club he originally intended to study ended in failure, despite his having the necessary props in terms of a customized high-performance motorcycle and the appropriate clothing. Trying to force the access process, he asked too many questions and fell foul of a biker who physically attacked him.

Hopper and Moore (1990) report being threatened with guns by a group of bikers who mistook them for members of a rival group. Bikers are contemptuous of outsiders and insist on deference from them. As a result, according to Hopper and Moore, researchers need to be careful about taking issue with group members. In their case, for example, a group of bikers became angry and threatening after one of the researchers made a mildly derogatory comment about a televised wrestling match the group had been watching. The need to avoid trouble and to remain sensitive to what might in other circumstances appear to be quite innocuous circumstances can make fieldwork a tense and precarious process. Moreover, when violent incidents do occur, they can have fateful consequences for the research. Having broken his assailant's thumb in the struggle produced by his inopportune questions, Wolf felt it necessary to move to another city to carry out his research. Patrick (1973), who undertook a covert study of a youth gang in Glasgow, records being taunted, jostled, and finally assaulted by a gang member who apparently resented his relationship to the gang's leader. He acquitted himself well in fighting off the assault, enhancing his reputation with the other gang members in the process. As in Wolf's case, however, the tension generated by the incident was instrumental in encouraging him to leave the field.

Hopper and Moore kept silent about aspects of the bikers' behavior they found personally objectionable, because they felt it would be dangerous to voice their opinions. The problem is more acute in covert studies. As Mitchell (1991) puts it, researchers "must do more than affirm the action, they must contribute to it" (p. 106). In other words, if one is not to be excluded, it is frequently necessary to talk and act in ways that are acceptable to those studied, even if they are at variance with one's personal values. Mitchell recounts an incident at a survivalist camp when he had to participate in a conversation in which the participants were expected to propose violently homophobic measures. In another example, the gang Patrick studied fought other gangs with hatchets and open razors. Patrick's reluctance to carry weapons and be actively involved in fighting was noticed by gang members and occasioned hostile comment from them.

Jankowski (1991) studied gangs in New York, Los Angeles, and Boston over a 10-year period. He notes that commonly, when he tried to gain access, gang members set two tests to assess his acceptability and trustworthiness. The first test was of a kind frequently set for researchers studying deviant behavior. Gang members would engage in illegal activities while Jankowski was with them, in order to see whether he would inform the authorities. On one occasion a gang member falsely accused him of informing the police about a crime the gang member had himself committed. As a result of this accusation Jankowski was attacked by gang members, although later, when the truth of the matter became known, the leadership of the gang apologized to him and allowed his study to go forward. The second test Jankowski usually faced involved gang members starting a fight with him. Such challenges, according to Jankowski, cannot be refused, although there is no disgrace—as in Patrick's case, mentioned earlier—in losing after putting up a fight. In some cases, fighting in this way served as an initiation ritual, but Jankowski also points out that, from a functional point of view, such fights provide an indication of whether a newcomer will be an asset or a liability in a confrontation with members of a rival gang. Jankowski seems to have coped quite well with these altercations. Having participated in gangs while growing up in Detroit, and being trained in karate, he was obviously able to look after himself. Yet, his rather throwaway admission that he "was only seriously injured twice" (1991, p. 12) might be twice too often for many other researchers.

Studies of these groups can also lead to difficulties in disseminating research findings. Patrick published under a pseudonym because of legal difficulties associated with the violence he observed. Wolf records opposition to the publication of his thesis in book form. A police officer appearing for the prosecution in a case involving a biker claimed the status of expert witness on the basis of having read Wolf's thesis. As a result, the biker felt that he had a score to settle with Wolf; and even though the biker was eventually mollified, Wolf acknowledges that going ahead with publication was potentially dangerous. Adler and Adler (1993) contend that ethnographers commonly suppress writing on particular topics, or they omit relevant materials from portrayals of those they study. Among the reasons Adler and Adler identify for self-censorship of this kind is the fear that research participants may take reprisals if material published about them is not to their liking. Fears of this kind have emerged in a number of contexts. According to Adler and Adler (1993), for instance, Mitchell had qualms about publishing material on the survivalists he studied. While Gambetta (1993) published a detailed study of the Sicilian Mafia, he took care to ensure that its publication would remain free of repercussions. Gambetta argues that organized crime groups are suspicious of situations in which information about them is released in piecemeal form, because they do not know whether further and possibly damaging information will emerge at a later date. To avoid this problem, Gambetta did not give interviews to journalists while his book was being written. Furthermore, on its publication he went on record (Griffiths, 1993) as saying that all the information he gathered is contained in the book, and he does not intend to produce a sequel.

5. OCCUPATIONAL HAZARDS

Fitzpatrick makes the point that, although there are many studies of occupations and of occupational stress, few of them explore how workers in dangerous occupations cope with the hazards they face. Even fewer, as will be seen, explore how researchers deal with hazards in sites that double as workplaces for them and for those they research. A number of factors help to insulate those researching work and occupations from potential danger. First, many of the major theoretical concerns in the sociology of work and occupations—issues such as skilling and deskilling, alienation, the impact of technology, the labor process, and so on—have encouraged the study of production line jobs notable more for their routine and repetitive character than for the hazards associated with them. One can also note that, often for political reasons, covert studies of work have also mainly focused on production line jobs. (For a brief summary of such studies, see Beynon, 1988.) Second, in the case of many industrial hazards—exposure to carcinogenic chemicals, for instance—it is the consequences of long-term exposure that are dangerous. While researchers involved in overt studies usually spend long periods with workers both on and off the job, their involvement in the work process itself and its possible dangers is usually peripheral or negligible. In a similar way, in areas such as studies of sports professionals who are at some risk of injury, researchers do not share those risks, because factors such as age and their own lack of skill render them ineligible for participation (see, e.g., Adler & Adler, 1991; Gallmeier, 1991).

It is perhaps not surprising therefore that where the issue of danger to the researcher has been raised in studies of work it has been in occupations that Goffman terms "fatefully consequential" (1977, p. 171), occupations where participants consciously place themselves at risk in problematic circumstances. As Goffman observes, the ability to successfully conduct a risky enterprise of this type carries with it evaluations of moral worth. Fieldworkers may therefore find, as Haas (1977) did, that such evaluations are extended to them, even when they have had little opportunity to prepare for the particular combination of fate and consequence they are asked to face.

Haas studied high steel ironworkers, construction workers who erect the steel skeleton supporting tall buildings. The ironworkers work in all types of weather, high up on the structure, walking and handling heavy loads on narrow steel beams. Haas describes arriving at a 21-story office building under construction for his first day of fieldwork. That was when he first realized that to do the research, he would have to take his place alongside the workers on the top of the building:

> But as I looked up, I knew I was not prepared for this. These were the people I had come to study and they were up there, and as I watched them I was dumbfounded and awe-struck by their aplomb. They "ran the iron" with seeming abandon. It was apparent from the ground that workers moving so confidently across and up and down the beams were unafraid. (1977, p. 150)

Although he confesses to having been in a state of "controlled terror," Haas made his way up the structure, attempting as best he could to maintain his poise, feeling that to do otherwise might inhibit rapport with the ironworkers. Eventually Haas realized that he was acting as the ironworkers did. Just as he concealed his fear from them, so they concealed their fear from each other. To do otherwise was to cast doubt on the extent to which they could be trusted in a dangerous situation.

There are relatively few occupations where the discrepancy between outward calm and inner turmoil is likely to be as great as it was for Haas. However, putting on a brave face—literally—may also be a requirement for studying occupational groups such as the police. A recurrent theme in police research is the boring and uneventful character of much routine police work. Nevertheless, car chases, brawls, and other disturbances all contain an element of risk for police officers and participant observers accompanying them (Manning, 1972). There have been situations, as Manning indicates, where police officers have maneuvered researchers into what might be called the "Uriah position," after the biblical story in which King David had Uriah the Hittite placed at the point in the line of battle where the danger was greatest. More often, however, potential risks are taken to be symbolically inclusive for both police and researchers, but actual exposure to danger is operationally distributed. To put this another way, police researchers are often expected to display, through demeanor or verbal commitment, that they can be relied on to "do the right thing" in a tight spot. In practice, however, an implicit research bargain emerges, in which the fieldworker plays conscript to the police officer's Marine. So the researcher has to be brave enough not to run away when trouble looms, but is charged for the most part with nothing more demanding than securing the rear, blocking retreats, and guarding the prisoners. This allocation of researchers to the margins of risk may also occur even when danger emerges unexpectedly. Punch (1979), for example, observes that any inclination toward heroics that he might have had was thwarted by his own slowness and indecision. Typically, the moment of danger had passed before he had collected his thoughts sufficiently to do anything about it. (Punch is not alone in recording his less-than-optimum performance when confronted with the actual mechanics of police work. See also, e.g., Pepinsky, 1980; Van Maanen, 1988.)

Researchers face obvious risks when they study dangerous occupations. It is precisely these risks, such as falling to one's death off a high structure or confronting a hostile and potentially deadly adversary, that loom large in comparison with other more mundane ways of earning a living. This rather dramatic contrast should not, however, disguise the potential hazards to be found more widely in the study of workers and workplace relations. It is not unusual for researchers who enter firms or organizations to face suspicion or hostility from workers or pressure from managements to pass on information about union activity (on this last see, e.g., Argyris, 1952; Beynon, 1988). The situation grows somewhat more difficult where the workplace becomes the site of open and sometimes violent conflict. Recounting his experiences while studying union organizing tactics, Roy (1970) points out that in these circumstances research is by no means free of danger. Just as in the kinds of conflict situations described earlier, concerns emerge about the identity and allegiance of the researcher. Roy, for instance, describes an occasion when he was confronted in a threatening manner by a group of workers attempting to enforce a strike, and was able to escape assault only by demonstrating that he was known to the local union organizer.

Roy's account also provides a reminder that the confrontations that take place on picket lines or at demonstrations are not devoid of at least minor hazard. Researching such events poses a number of problems. The activities of those present, including the researcher, are visible and open to scrutiny for what they might reveal about individual sympathies. For example, on another occasion Roy found himself with a group of strikers who were stoning the cars of strikebreakers after their police escort had withdrawn from the site of the dispute. Roy, who combined sympathy for the strikers with a tough-minded commitment to dispassionate observation, was not prepared to join in the stone throwing; however, neither did he wish the strikers to view him as being unenthusiastic about their cause. He goes on to describe how he salved his conscience, producing in the process one of the more surreal images in industrial sociology:

> I made my decision. Sweating freely—it was a warm night—I ran back and forth with the strikers, stooping and swaying and swinging my arms in a balletic imitation of a man throwing rocks. Finally the last car screamed around the bend in the road. With my companions I made a rapid but dignified dash for my own automobile. The cops did not show up. (1970, p. 242)

A further difficulty for those involved in picket lines and the like is that the ecology of such events means that the point of confrontation must actively be sought out by the researcher if it is to be observed (Fischer, 1972). The turbulence of collective behavior, however, also sometimes propels toward confrontation even those, including researchers, who do not wish to be there, as examples from areas other than industrial disputes make clear. Stephen Small, whose arrest at a demonstration was described earlier, fell over an obstruction and found himself on the wrong side of police lines. Despite his obvious nonhostile intent, Small was seized and taken away. Getting too close to the action, in this case with a video camera, may also have produced the injury sustained by

Nick Fiddes (Wojtas, 1994). Fiddes, an anthropologist studying hunt saboteurs (the British term for animal rights activists who directly attempt to disrupt hounds and riders engaged in foxhunting), was allegedly kicked in the face by a huntsman when he videotaped a fox being caught by hounds.

6. SEXUAL HARASSMENT AND ASSAULT

Despite an increasing openness about experiences in the field in recent years, the risks female social scientists face in doing research remain underdocumented (Warren, 1988). Unwillingness to discuss sexual matters in print has muted discussion concerning the extent to which female researchers are subjected to sexual harassment or assault within the research setting (Warren, 1988, pp. 37-38; Whitehead & Price, 1986). Whitehead notes a "plethora of stories" concerning sexual relations in the field, which include instances of sexual extortion and/or rapes (or attempts) by host country informants, colleagues, or supervisors, but hazards no estimate of the size of the problem (Whitehead & Price, 1986). Stanko (1992) polled members of the women and crime division of the American Society of Criminology about their experiences of sexual harassment. Close to one in three of those who responded reported being subjected during fieldwork to sexual comments or harassing behavior from police officers, prison officers, and court officials—including judges. The response rate on Stanko's survey was rather low. Even if one makes the (implausible) assumption that none of the nonresponders had encountered harassment, Stanko's work, however, suggests that sexual harassment encountered during fieldwork is a far from insignificant problem.

Reports of rape or attempted rape were given by 7% of the women in Howell's (1990) sample of anthropologists. She adds, however, "it is a touchy subject, and one that I am quite sure is under-reported in the sample" (p. 94). Howell further suggests that sexual assault is a greater danger for fieldworkers in some locations than in others. She points in particular to North Africa and parts of East Africa, New Guinea, and some Latin American countries, although she notes that fieldworkers in some regions, notably the Middle East, disagree sharply about the dangers faced by female anthropologists (see, e.g., Nader, 1986).

Golde (1986) argues that female anthropologists entering the field must typically confront cultural expectations both about female vulnerability and about what constitutes safe conduct. Such expectations are typically based on assumptions that women are weak, naive, unresourceful, and, in some settings, sexually provocative. Assumptions of this kind, Golde points out, are often transformed into a fabric of solicitousness directed at channeling the fieldworker into appropriate situations, relationships, and residence. For example, the fieldworker might acquire local protectors of various kinds or be taken under the wing of a local family. Not infrequently female ethnographers are assigned roles that either minimize or neutralize their sexual status or are traditionally protected within the culture. In some cases, they might also be expected to restrict their activities to the sphere of women and children, or to work with a husband or as part of a team of researchers.

Golde does not see this in an entirely negative light. In her view, communal solicitousness toward the fieldworker, especially at times of crisis, can be emotionally gratifying to the researcher, as well as symbolically demonstrating community commitment to her well-being. As Golde stresses, however, concerns about fieldworker safety often also represent a latent form of social control, constraining the researcher's actions and limiting her freedom to maneuver. Nor is social control operating under the guise of protectiveness solely a prerogative of those within the research setting. It may also operate in academic and administrative circles, shaping the research topics and settings typically open to female researchers. Lutkehaus (1986) documents, for example, how early British male social anthropologists cited the likelihood of sexual assault as a reason for excluding female anthropologists from fieldwork, revealing in the process more about their own racial and gender stereotypes than about the actual fieldwork situation.

Female researchers in organizations frequently encounter a pattern of gender roles that assigns them to marginal or subordinate roles as "mascots" or "gofers" (Easterday, Papademas, Schorr, & Valentine, 1977). They may also have to contend in the workplace with sexual comments, jokes, and innuendo. While male, liberal-minded researchers have on occasion been embarrassed by such activities (Gallmeier, 1991; Morgan, 1972), they are less likely to feel threatened by them than female researchers. Drawing on Kanter's (1977) analysis of women in male-dominated organizations, Gurney (1985) suggests that sexual banter of this kind is often used as a loyalty test, designed to see how the female researcher will react. Although there is apparently some variability, depending on sex ratio, organizational culture, and perhaps also the nature of the research (Easterday et al., 1977; Gurney, 1991), it is not infrequent that female researchers report instances of sexual hustling by research participants. Easterday et al., for instance, provide as an example an extract from an interview transcript in which the questions put by a female fieldworker to a male informant are assiduously parried by requests for information about her availability. Advances can also be used as a method of controlling the data collection process. Daniels (1967, p. 270) notes that the army officers she studied sometimes evaded her questions by responding to them in a "frankly seductive manner." Gurney (1991) suggests that problems of this kind can sometimes be dealt with by private diplomacy, at least where this does not produce vulnerability. She also suggests approaching others in the setting with whom one has established rapport for advice and possible intervention.

A number of writers (Gurney, 1985; Warren, 1988) have argued that there is often, in effect, a trade-off for female researchers between being treated in a demeaning or sexually predatory way and gathering the data they require from the setting. Published accounts of fieldwork by female researchers reveal, they suggest, a range of attitudes toward this trade-off. Some researchers treat the matter as a necessary evil. Ackers (1993) speaks, for instance, of the "bitter fee" of access. Others find the trade-off personally and politically distasteful. According to writers like Warren and Gurney, however, female fieldworkers are frequently silent about how they actually deal with the conflict between information gathering and the offensive behavior of research participants. Warren suggests that for a variety of reasons such behavior is either tolerated or at least not fully acknowledged in published writing. Researchers may be embarrassed to recount untoward incidents, or may blame themselves for permitting such situations to arise. Fieldworkers, Warren contends, are often grateful to those they study for having allowed access to the setting in the first place and in many instances fear that acting in a forceful or assertive way will damage rapport. In some cases, the researcher may be unwilling to discredit those being studied by revealing negative information about them, particularly if in doing so they risk confirming negative stereotypes of the group under study. There are also career concerns. Taking Gurney's (1985) point that work by female researchers may be undervalued by professional audiences, Warren speculates that female researchers may seek to conceal fieldwork difficulties, especially those relating to gender, for fear of harming their career prospects.

Howell (1990) suggests that female anthropologists working at remote sites can be in a vulnerable position because they are outside protective networks, even if only temporarily, and may be unaware of the signals of challenge and deference with which local women protect themselves (p. 93). In urban contexts, female researchers may be vulnerable both in public places and in private spaces. Dorothy Douglas (1972), who studied a commercial ambulance service, speaks of her fear of attack on being driven to a secluded spot late at night by a driver who was hostile to the research. (In the event, he used the occasion to express his fear that she was a management spy.) Daniels (1967) found that her male respondents sometimes misinterpreted her willingness to collect data outside of office hours as an expression of sexual availability. McKee and O'Brien (1983) point to the potential vulnerability of female researchers interviewing men about intimate matters. They experienced few difficulties in a study of new fathers, though even here one respondent adopted a rather predatory stance toward the researcher. In their study of lone fathers, McKee and O'Brien deliberately chose not to discuss sexual matters directly with their respondents. Nevertheless, in a number of interviews the issue arose in ways that made the interviewer fearful of attack. As they put it:

> Neither of us experienced physical abuse throughout our research with men, although in two cases in the lone fathers project the interviewer began to feel worried about possible attack and in two cases was pestered after the interview for further contact. In these interviews the researcher employed a variety of strategies to offset any risk of sexual confrontation: taking conscious decisions about make-up and clothes; and maintaining a "professional" manner when ambiguities arose. The props on these occasions were things rather than people: the tape-recorder, the clip-board and interview schedule—although the presence of children and others was also a mediating factor. (1983, pp. 157-158)

Research with deviant groups may require female researchers to operate in locales or at times that potentially render them vulnerable to attack or to importuning advances. Dunlap developed cordial nonresearch-based relations with a number of local drug dealers who reciprocated by adopting a protective role toward her when she needed to move through the area late at night (Williams et al., 1992). Crack users, under the influence of the drug, may make sexual advances to others in the setting, including the researcher (Williams et al., 1992, pp. 355, 363). It seems that such advances can be fairly easily evaded, discouraged, or deflected onto willing participants. According to Williams et al., in low-income communities where foster care or attenuated kinship ties are common, ethnographers sometimes become treated as fictive kin. This can have a protective function as a female member of their research team, Eloise Dunlap, records:

> Smoking crack causes many individuals to be stimulated sexually. Yet when first developing rapport, potential subjects frequently assign a fictive-kin role. I may seem like a sister, cousin, mother or aunt to them. Assuming such roles leads individuals to become "close friends" and share many behaviors they would not otherwise exhibit. When projecting such roles to me, they place me "off limits" for sexual approaches and affairs. (Williams et al., 1992, p. 363)

During her research with gang members Horowitz (1986) discovered in a similar way that her age and education placed her off limits. Initially unsure of her identity, the gang members she studied eventually defined her as a "lady reporter." As such, they avoided discussing sexual matters with her, much less making sexual advances. Through time, however, she increasingly came to be defined as an insider. As this happened, the volume of sexual teasing increased, as did attempts to define her as available for sexual relations. To circumvent this situation, Horowitz eventually withdrew from spending time with male gang members in favor of studying young women in the neighborhood.

Female researchers have sometimes been accepted into a research setting with rather less suspicion than might have greeted a male colleague (Golde, 1986, p. 8). Though not inevitably the case (see, e.g., Brewer, 1993), women can be perceived as less of a threat than men in a situation of violent conflict. According to Milroy (1980), who carried out sociolinguistic research in three areas of Belfast, the fieldworker on her project "had to be a woman." She explains: "Women were much less likely to be attacked than men, and since male strangers were at that time viewed with considerable suspicion in many parts of Belfast, they were likely to be in some danger if they visited one place over a protracted period" (p. 44).

Moreover, she points out, the researcher had to work alone in the setting she studied. Because a woman working on her own was less threatening than a man or a team of researchers, it was possible to stay in a particular area longer and thus collect more data. Although the areas she worked in posed very clear dangers to the researcher's physical security, Milroy does not mention the possibility of sexual assault. This may be because rates of reported crime unrelated to the conflict—including sexual offenses—are quite low in Northern Ireland. An additional factor is that scrutiny of public spaces is common in the kinds of traditional working-class areas Milroy studied. It is more than likely that scrutiny of this kind has increased as a result of the conflict.

7. INVOLUNTARY RESEARCH

Adler and Adler (1987) distinguish three types of membership role that field researchers can assume in research situations: the peripheral, the active, and the complete. They further subdivide the category of complete membership into two subtypes: Opportunistic researchers study settings of which they are already members; converts enter a research setting as outsiders but eventually become inducted into full membership. It is possible to add a third, if somewhat rare, subtype to the Adlers' typology of complete membership roles: the involuntary participant. These are researchers who observe a situation they have been condemned—sometimes literally—to enter.

One famous example of involuntary research is Bruno Bettelheim's (1961) observation of the Nazi concentration camps. Bettelheim was arrested in 1938 and incarcerated in the concentration camps of Dachau and Buchenwald until his release and subsequent emigration to the United States in 1939. Bettelheim's work has been controversial. It has been criticized for its lack of historical perspective (Davidowicz, 1981, p. 178) and for its apparent suggestion that inmates passively accepted their fate (De Pres, 1976). What is at issue here, however, is the method Bettelheim used, not his conclusions. Bettelheim comments that it was self-interest rather than scientific curiosity that encouraged him to observe his own behavior and that of others while he was in the camp. After a time he became aware that observation might help him avoid mental disintegration. It occupied his time, enabled him to feel he was doing something constructive, and allowed him to escape mentally from his surroundings.

Observation in the camp was supremely difficult. Taking notes was an impossibility. Bettelheim had to train himself to memorize what he saw, which was hampered by the effects of malnutrition. Only after emigration and his return to health did much of what he had temporarily forgotten come back to him. Outside of a few brief periods at mealtimes and at the end of the day, opportunities to talk to other prisoners were limited. At other times talking was forbidden. Nevertheless, prisoners talked when they could because it eased the burden of their physical labor. Moreover, there was no particular benefit from adhering to the rule, because prisoners quickly discovered that compliance was no protection against arbitrary punishment. The SS unwittingly facilitated Bettelheim's observations. They moved prisoners from work detail to work detail to prevent the growth of solidarity among the inmates. This meant that Bettelheim was able to observe many different situations and to speak to many different people. He was able to check his impressions and observations with two other inmates whose interests and backgrounds were similar to his own.

In such settings too great an involvement in the research role can be dangerous. First, in some extreme situations, constant vigilance is necessary for survival. Observation may serve to fatally draw one's attention away from the situation at hand. Second, observation is potentially a threat to those with power in the setting. As Bettelheim (1961) records, the concentration camps contained "an impressive lesson that said: you may notice only what we wish you to notice, but you invite death if you notice things on your own volition" (p. 154). Unless by threats or exhortation the SS explicitly drew their attention to an atrocity, concentration camp inmates deliberately avoided watching another prisoner's mistreatment for fear of drawing attention to themselves.

Opportunistic researchers and potential converts face hard-to-resist pressures toward role immersion (Adler & Adler, 1987, p. 73). For involuntary researchers, as Bettelheim realized, role immersion can be potentially fatal. In the extreme situation of the concentration camp, observation became, in Goffman's (1961) terms, a secondary adjustment: "any habitual arrangement by which a member of an organization employs unauthorized means, or obtains unauthorized ends, or both, thus getting around the organization's assumptions as to what he should do and get and hence what he should be" (p. 172). Involuntary research documents the indignities and cruelties associated with total institutions and extreme situations. It also provides psychological prophylaxis. These features combine to exempt the involuntary observer from the ethical strictures that normally surround covert research (see, e.g., Bulmer, 1982a).

8. REDUCING RISK

Having documented the extent to which ethnographers suffer illness, injury, and, on occasion, death in the field, Howell (1990, p. 192) echoes C. Wright Mills in observing that events experienced as burdens or tragedies at a personal level represent classes of problem when viewed from a wider perspective. She goes on, therefore, to make a number of suggestions and recommendations about improving health and safety in the field. On a practical level, she stresses the importance of being able to summon help or to leave the setting in the event of an emergency. In particular, she suggests that researchers working in remote areas should investigate the usefulness of devices such as two-way radios, emergency beacons, and cellular telephones for use in emergencies. This point has also been strongly made by Kulick (1991), reporting an encounter with bandits in Papua New Guinea in which an informant was murdered (but see Lipset, 1993). Kulick urges researchers in remote locations to equip themselves with shortwave radios and rapid transportation so that they can summon help if need be. A difficulty in relying on technological devices is that they may be too complicated to be readily used in an emergency. Howell provides an instance of radio equipment, left unpacked because of the effort required to set it up, which was then unavailable for use when needed. (Situations of this kind affect not just remote sites. According to Norris, 1990, personal attack alarms issued to staff in a social work agency in the United Kingdom were so sophisticated that few people learned to operate them properly.) In addition, in the kind of hostile situation described by Kulick, there is presumably a risk of inviting preemptive attempts to render communication devices inoperable. (Howell, 1990, makes a similar point about the ownership of guns.) According to Sluka (1990), researchers should recognize that they may need to terminate the research abruptly and accept that, under certain conditions, it might be terminated by others. In some settings, the ability to leave the setting quickly may mean little more than having sufficient funds for a plane ticket. In others the logistics may be more difficult. For example, the researcher who seeks emergency evacuation in the case of urgent medical need may have to establish in advance a line of monetary credit with the appropriate evacuation body (Howell, 1990, p. 187).

Safety Awareness

Beyond emergency preparedness Howell (1990, p. 185) argues the need for a greater awareness of safety in social research as a matter of *normative* practice. Present attitudes, she claims, too often support a culture of denial. For instance, she notes that many of the anthropologists who responded to her survey remarked on the unsympathetic stance taken by departmental colleagues in response to accounts of difficulties and dangers faced during fieldwork (1990, p. 190). Responses of this kind are not confined to anthropology. In sociology, Brahuja and Hallowell (1986) comment that colleagues can easily come to resent what they perceive as illegitimate demands for emotional support, especially when these come from junior colleagues or graduate students. More generally, social definitions of danger in sociology are embedded in the moral tales expressed in first-person accounts of the field research process, or in "corridor talk" (Warren, 1988). These sources are often suffused by images of "asceticism, anomie and atrocity" (Lee, 1992, p. 120), implicitly containing the message that fieldworkers are the kinds of people who can put up with constant and dedicated hard work, loneliness, powerlessness, confusion, and suffering at the hands of those being studied. Although these lessons are laudable in their own right, they have sometimes been given a rather fatalistic gloss. The first field experience in particular becomes a rite of passage, which the beginning fieldworker must traverse relatively unaided. In this situation researchers can be left more or less unprepared for the possible dangers that might confront them.

The form a greater awareness of safety issues might take is a potentially contentious matter. Anthropologists, for example, are unlikely to welcome an overly prescriptive approach. Traditionally, they have been unwilling to compromise the independence of the fieldworker, a concern expressed in a reluctance to prescribe graduate research methods courses. While acknowledging the importance of disciplinary sensibilities, Howell (1990) argues that much more can be done. First, she argues for greater availability of information. Obvious resources, information about health hazards, for example, should be readily accessible, preferably on a departmental basis. However, the need is not simply for more information, but for timely and accurate information. To this end, she suggests that it can often be most appropriate to coordinate the collection and dissemination of safety information at a regional level, or at the level of particular specialties. This is likely to ensure more timely and relevant information, although the obvious danger is that information may not diffuse more widely to groups elsewhere with similar needs. Howell also sees a need for professional associations to establish, where necessary, task forces to investigate particular hazards and take action to deal with them.

Related to the need for better information is a more explicit commitment to improving awareness of safety issues among graduate students. Howell argues that senior researchers should be more open about the kinds of dangers they faced in their research and the steps they took to overcome them. She also contends that what is passed on to graduate students as wisdom and lore about operating in the field is sometimes simply bad advice. A greater range of available information would help counter less than helpful advice.

Howell's (1990) survey, which by and large reflects North American practice, suggests that responsibility for informing graduate students of fieldwork dangers in anthropology is most often left to the supervisor. There is little in the way of formal policy for monitoring dangerous situations, reporting back on how students coped with them, or providing systematic training. Impressionistically, a similar situation obtains in sociology. Kulick (1991) suggests that supervisors have an obligation to advise and, if necessary, prevent graduate students from entering violent social settings unprepared. Although supervisors clearly do have ethical responsibilities toward students, a strongly restrictive regime may be inappropriate. A joint approach, in which supervisors and students jointly assess potential risks, seems preferable.

In Britain, universities have a legal duty to provide the supervision necessary to ensure both the health and the safety of undergraduate and postgraduate students (CVCP, 1993). This duty devolves onto individual supervisors, who must exercise an "effective supervisory role" in relation to students they supervise; they cannot simply assume a student's competence. In guidance recently given to universities, the Committee of Vice-Chancellors and Principals (CVCP), an advisory and consultative, but nevertheless authoritative, body within British higher education, recommends a system of risk assessment in which supervisors and students should agree on the level of risk inherent in particular research procedures, the level of supervision necessary, and the precautions that need to be taken. Four levels of risk are specified. The lowest is where risks are insignificant and students need no special supervision. Above this are research procedures that require extra care but where students have been trained and are competent to deal with the risks involved. At a higher level of risk are two further categories, one where work may not be started without the supervisor's advice and approval, the other where work may only be started with direct supervision. Adhering to the risk assessment procedure does not remove ultimate responsibility for safety from the university. Moreover, risk assessment in itself forms only part of the duties of supervisors in relation to health and safety. They are also required to provide information, instruction, and training where appropriate (CVCP, 1993, p. 3). Quite clearly, this system was formulated with laboratory sciences in mind. Probably the vast majority of research procedures in the social sciences fall into the "insignificant risks" category. There are presumably also few situations where social science research is so hazardous that it can only be carried out with permission or under direct supervision. Clearly, though, certain kinds of field research will be of a kind where extra care must be observed and where an assessment of the risks involved should be undertaken.

Funding

In addition to changes in departmental and supervisory practice, Howell advocates putting pressure on institutions, such as funding bodies, professional associations, universities, and government agencies, to give safety matters more serious consideration. Howell (1990) provides a gloomy assessment of the impact existing funding arrangements have on ensuring that health and safety in the field are not compromised. Because, as she argues, most kinds of social science research are in any case chronically underfunded, there seems little prospect of increasing grants to cover additional fieldwork costs related to safety considerations. Again, the problems here seem to be worst in anthropology. Although in urban contexts funds needed, for example, to buy alarms, cover taxi fares, or even hire escorts may be relatively modest, the potential safety costs involved in working at remote sites can sometimes be substantial. Since it is not uncommon in anthropology for researchers to bear in advance some of the cost of fieldwork themselves, there are clearly temptations to economize. In Howell's view, the issues become particularly difficult where researchers engaged in long-term fieldwork are accompanied in the field by their families. In these cases, Howell (1990, p. 188) contends, existing funding arrangements tend to produce two equally unpalatable choices. Either families and dependents have to be treated as ineligible for the safety benefits provided under the terms of the grant, or the available facilities are diluted to cover more people than were originally included in the budget.

Although Howell's observations ring true, it still needs to be said that assessments researchers make of funders' priorities are not always accurate. Indeed, in some cases self-fulfilling prophecies arise, in which researchers do not ask for appropriate funding simply because they assume it will not be available (Bell, 1984). There are some cases where funders are at least aware of safety issues. The Economic and Social Research Council, which, through its Training Board, provides the major source of funding for graduate students in the social sciences in the United Kingdom, treats safety matters as first and foremost a matter for supervisors and departments. As a matter of policy, however, the Board is prepared to look sympathetically at particular cases where safety concerns legitimately place demands on student resources. That said, a more systematic assessment of the attitudes funding agencies have toward health and safety issues would be useful. It would make possible the kind of pressure Howell argues is necessary to raise the consciousness of funders about potential fieldwork dangers.

Policy Issues

In examining the policies institutions have for dealing with fieldwork hazard, two different institutional contexts can be distinguished. On the one hand, there are field-staffed organizations: research institutes, survey organizations, applied social research units, and the like. On the other, there are situations more typical of academic settings where researchers, working individually or in small teams, operate in effect as independent practitioners, who may nevertheless have responsibility toward students, colleagues, and administrators. Turning first to situations of the latter kind, there seems to be considerable variation in the extent to which universities and related bodies have put internal policies into place with regard to fieldwork (Howell, 1990, p. 191). These range from a laissez-faire approach; through one which recognizes that geologists, biologists, and the like do field research but ignores social scientists; to situations where a fully developed safety policy is in place. Insofar as there is a trend, Howell suggests that, in North America at least, it is toward a greater awareness of safety issues on the part of university administrators. However, she attributes this awareness to increasing concerns about liability and insurance cover.

There is no systematic information on the arrangements researchers make about insurance. A typical arrangement common to a number of countries seems to be that university staff are covered by insurance, provided they have obtained the necessary leave of absence from their institution. However, there seems to be variation between institutions and between countries concerning the extent of coverage. Although some institutions cover staff for direct physical loss or damage to university-owned equipment, personal accident and third-party liability worldwide, others will not insure equipment taken overseas. In addition, coverage frequently does not extend to students and nonemployees of the university. Special insurance arrangements may therefore need to be made when students are taken into the field, or research assistants are hired locally.

Researchers who work in hazardous environments may have problems relying on institutional cover. Researchers on the police have in some situations had to sign waivers of liability in order to gain access (N. Fielding, personal communication), while at least one university has been dropped by an insurance company following a fieldwork-related claim (M. Fischer, personal communication). Standard insurance policies typically exclude risks deriving from war, political turmoil, and the like. Fieldwork in particular regions may, therefore, require additional and expensive cover, producing the temptation to skimp on coverage precisely in the kinds of situation where it is of most use.

Concerns about liability have encouraged a trend toward a more explicit acknowledgment of the risks involved in fieldwork. Implicit in this trend is an assumption that researchers should undertake research in risky environments on the basis of their own informed consent (see, e.g., University of Toronto, 1988). Informed consent has an important, and in some countries legally enshrined, role in ensuring the protection of human subjects from harm (Lee, 1993). Using the principle of informed consent to govern the research process can, however, have paradoxical consequences (Reiss, 1979). In many cases the person most informed about potential hazards is actually the researcher. Researchers are not, however, disinterested parties. They may be tempted to minimize potential risks in order to ensure that the research goes ahead. In this way, informed consent increases rather than diminishes possible exposure to hazard. Conversely, liability considerations tend to make institutions risk-averse. Requiring researchers to give informed consent may be a means of shifting liability from the institution onto the individual.

Employers do, of course, have legal obligations to their employees. The question is how far these obligations extend beyond laboratory facilities, for example, to the kinds of hazardous settings likely to be frequented by social scientists. Moves toward deregulation are currently under way, but at the moment employers in the United Kingdom have a responsibility under the Health and Safety at Work Act (1974) for providing "as far as is reasonably practicable" a safe and healthy workplace. They also have a duty to provide appropriate safety training. It has been assumed that these responsibilities extend to protecting employees who come into contact with the public from the possibility of physical assault (Brown, Bute, & Ford, 1986). Conceivably, the corresponding statute in the United States, the Occupational Safety and Health Act (OSHA), could also be interpreted in this way. However, the U.S. courts have not considered whether OSHA does lay upon employers a statutory duty to protect employees from assault by a third party. It seems in general that judgments about an employer's liability hinge on whether a danger in the workplace could have reasonably been foreseen. In cases relating, for example, to the liability of a landlord, where a tenant has been attacked in the hallway of the landlord's apartment building, the unpredictability of the attack has been taken to imply that it could not have reasonably been anticipated. It is an open question whether this reasoning would be accepted in court in situations where a researcher, as an employee, operated in an environment that routinely posed a threat of interpersonal violence.

Field-Staffed Organizations

Traditionally, field-staffed organizations have been oriented to quantitative research. The increased legitimacy of qualitative methods in areas like evaluation research (Patton, 1987) or AIDS intervention research (Kotarba, 1990) means, however, that ethnographers increasingly find themselves in staff positions in such organizations. Possible dangers to survey research staff have been obviated to a degree by the increasing use of telephone, as opposed to face-to-face, interviewing. Ethnographic field staff cannot, of course, mediate their relationship to the field in this way. They must enter the settings they study and face the risks they find there.

Where they exist at all, institutional responses to fieldwork dangers in field-staffed organizations take a variety of forms: precautionary guidelines; policy frameworks that specify good practice not just at field level, but in terms of managerial responsibilities; and the provision of training. Providing field staff with safety guidelines seems to have become increasingly common. Guidelines provided by a number of research organizations in both the United States and the United Kingdom were inspected during the preparation of this volume. Typically, they have a rather precautionary tone. Codifying in many ways a number of safety strategies already discussed, guidelines usually provide advice on maintaining contact with the field office and with other staff, the use of transport and accommodation in potentially insecure areas, the conduct of interviews, and behavior in an emergency. In each case, stress is placed on knowing the location of field staff at all times, the importance of sizing up fieldwork locales and situations, ensuring the availability of backup or support in potentially vulnerable situations, and the need for speedy exit in case of trouble.

Although guidelines probably do help to protect fieldworkers, their use is problematic in a number of respects. They can, for example, conflict with other responsibilities the researcher may have. Most obviously, a common stipulation, keeping others informed about one's whereabouts, may jeopardize the confidentiality of research participants if interpreted too literally. In research organizations, precautionary guidelines can also devolve onto the fieldworker a responsibility that properly lies with research managers. Another way to put this is that guidelines need to operate within a wider policy framework that ensures that the risks inherent in fieldwork are not compounded by managerial insistence that returns from data collection are maximized. Thus, in one example that stands as a model of good practice, a research institute in the United Kingdom has developed guidelines that explicitly set out the responsibility of the organization for ensuring the safety of staff, the responsibility of senior staff and supervisors for ensuring that the guidelines are disseminated and followed, as well as a commitment by the organization to supply equipment such as portable telephones or personal alarms where appropriate. Researchers are also reminded to budget for safety items when preparing research proposals. In a similar way, survey interviewers employed by the U.S. Bureau of the Census are explicitly instructed that reluctance to enter a potentially dangerous situation is an acceptable reason for noncompletion of an interview, and that two fieldworkers will not be sent into a situation regarded as too dangerous for one.

A further weakness of guidelines is that, in stressing the avoidance of trouble, they often ignore what happens *after* an unpleasant or dangerous incident. Accounts by doctors, social workers, and the like, who were attacked in the course of their work, suggest that professional workers frequently experience guilt at having been assaulted (Brown et al., 1986). Commonly, for such individuals, being attacked throws into doubt their feelings of professional competence. The incident provokes questions about who was at fault, whether the assault could have been avoided, or whether approaching the situation in a different way would have yielded a different outcome. In general, fieldworkers have little protection from the emotional stresses of carrying out research on topics that are painful or harrowing to informants (Brannen, 1988). Researchers operating in hazardous contexts, or who have endured unpleasant experiences while in the field, similarly have little protection. Brannen contrasts the position of researchers with that of other professionals—psychiatrists, therapists, counselors—for whom work-related stress is an occupational hazard. Often they are able to reduce the pressures involved by practicing on their own territory and at a time of their own choosing. They also often have available to them institutional sources of training and therapeutic intervention. As Brannen points out, social researchers who experience stress or trauma as the result of their research typically turn for support to others like themselves. Clearly, such a remedy is difficult where researchers operate as "lone hands," work at remote sites, or, as is often the case with graduate students, their existing professional networks are relatively truncated. Clearly, too, relying on co-workers may be insufficient in cases, for example, of sexual assault where specialist counseling may be needed.

Training

Reflecting on their experience of developing training methods to help social workers cope with violent incidents, Brown et al. (1986) make an important point. Often, the skills necessary to deal with danger are already in place and being exercised by experienced staff. Such skills are rarely shared or discussed, however, and as such fail to become disseminated. Effective training harnesses existing expertise and makes it widely available. In the course of a study of crack distribution, Williams et al. (1992) explicitly trained field staff on the dangers involved in drug-related research. Although they do not discuss their training methods in detail, it is clear that they relied heavily on the accumulated wisdom and experience of senior project members. In a different context, but with broadly similar intent, survey interviewers working for the U.S. Bureau of the Census view as part of their training a videotaped discussion between experienced field supervisors about the safety issues they face in a variety of locales, from inner cities to remote rural areas.

Especially where field staff risk physical violence, relying on the expertise of experienced staff has its limits. At best a superb tool for raising consciousness, at worst it may simply render what are in effect precautionary guidelines into a more obviously—if authoritative—didactic form. As Brown et al. (1986) comment, "The objective of training must always be to extend . . . competence towards the relatively small number of occasions when things go wrong" (p. 128). This implies that field staff should have the opportunity to develop and practice the skills involved in recognizing, preventing, and coping with dangerous situations. Staff may also, as Brown et al. point out, need opportunities to discharge their anxieties about the risks they face. A more developed approach to training would therefore embody the use of materials such as videotaped vignettes, for example showing the development of a violent incident, role-playing exercises, and open-ended discussion.

Video has the advantage of being a dynamic medium, well suited to the display of an unfolding social situation. Videotape can also be stopped, started, and rewound in ways that give the trainer close control over the material presented. Unless one can adapt readily existing materials, however, video production can be costly and requires professional assistance if a quality product is to be produced. Role playing, by contrast, is a cheap and readily accessible vehicle for simulating hazardous situations. Some writers have cautioned against its use, however, in cases where potentially violent incidents are to be enacted (Brown et al., 1986; Norris, 1990; see also Barnes, 1979, p. 131). The fear is that in role playing, such incidents can get out of hand and lead to actual emotional or physical harm to participants. Van Ments (1983), a noted proponent of the technique, argues that fears of "emotional escalation" in role-plays are exaggerated, although he does concede that there must always be remedial strategies available to deal with situations that go awry.

The impact of training needs to be carefully monitored. Used unwisely, training materials can actually increase fears or can make people overconfident about their ability to deal with the unexpected. To date, however, there is a lack of explicit evaluation of the extent to which training reduces dangers or makes field staff feel more secure.

9. CONCLUSION

Warren (1988) notes: "The fieldworker's reception by the host society is a reflection of the cultural contextualization of the fieldworker's characteristics, which include . . . ethnic, racial, class or national differences as well as gender" (p. 13). Fieldworkers need to be acutely sensitive to such contextualizations. Even in relatively tranquil contexts they can easily be transformed into designations such as insider, outsider, spy, victim, neutral, ally, or friend. Where fieldwork is dangerous because of the possibility of violence, negative characterizations of the fieldworker go beyond issues of acceptance or rejection to the possibility of direct physical harm to the researcher. Fortunately the dynamics of fieldwork situations are such that fieldworkers can often find and maintain, if only precariously, a role perceived as nonthreatening by those within the setting.

Johnson (1975) points out that entry to a field setting would be unproblematic if the researcher already possessed a detailed theoretical understanding of its social organization. Such an understanding can only be attained, however, by entering the setting and carrying out the research. One conclusion Johnson draws from this paradox is the need for researchers to undertake, as far as possible, a detailed preliminary reconnaissance of the field situation before attempting to enter it. Reconnaissance of this kind, where it is possible, is invaluable in dangerous settings. Moreover, at least for environmental and health hazards, the necessary information is frequently available. Prior assessment of the possible human hazards of research in particular settings is more difficult. As indicated earlier, some sources such as the media may need to be discounted, but knowledgeable insiders, area experts, and the like can all be sought out for specific knowledge of local conditions. Increased awareness of safety issues in research may also help by encouraging a greater sharing of relevant fieldwork experience.

Researchers working in dangerous settings are presumably most vulnerable early on in their field experience. This is because they are unlikely to have the degree of situational awareness that makes setting members competent at assessing potential dangers. Fortunately, in becoming culturally competent, the ethnographer also acquires the skills necessary to become aware of danger. Indeed, the offering of advice on coping with possible dangers may in itself indicate acceptance of the researcher, as might offers of protection or sanctuary. There is, however, an issue about whether safety skills can be acquired in more formal ways through training. As previously seen, training to deal with potential fieldwork hazard is already a feature of some areas of applied social research. However, in these situations potential hazards and ways of dealing with them are already likely to be well known, and pertinent expertise and support are often on hand. Apart from relevant disciplinary concerns about the character of fieldwork education (Howell, 1990), the wider availability of formal safety training may have only limited utility. At the same time, it is difficult to escape the conclusion that more attention should be paid, particularly within graduate education, to potential safety hazards and ways of dealing with them.

In the fieldwork literature the establishment of trust between researcher and researched is frequently seen as a condition for the establishment of good field relations. Some writers argue, however, that an emphasis on trust is misplaced. Douglas (1976), for example, sees it as the product of the "small-town, Protestant public morality of openness, friendliness and do-gooderism" typical of research in the Chicago tradition (p. 47). In his view much of what is worth knowing about social life is hidden from researchers behind a fabric of lies, evasions, misinformation, and fronts. If researchers are not to be duped by misleading self-presentations, Douglas argues, they need to take a more distrustful stance toward those they study, possibly by operating within the setting in a covert manner (see also Henslin, 1972). Paradoxically, covert research may be inadvisable precisely in those settings where there is no doubt that information is being hidden or that public fronts are highly misleading, as, for example, in the study of clandestine organizations found in situations of violent conflict or in organized crime. Covert researchers are vulnerable to mistakes and misunderstandings about who they are and what they are doing. Because some clandestine organizations combine an endemic concern about concealed identities with the use of violence as a routine protective device, misattributions can have deadly consequences.

Attempts to remedy unsatisfactory situations often fall into two traps. One involves the problem of "sensitization" (Cohen, 1972). What is taken to be problematic, once noticed, comes to be seen as everywhere. Apparent ubiquity, however, often invites disproportionate remedy. A second problem is that campaigns to increase awareness of hazards often ignore the culture of target groups (Davison, Frankel, & Smith, 1992). The kind of approach advocated by Howell (1990) is, therefore, a sensible one, as is the way she frames her recommendations in terms of the wider professional culture and institutional framework within which fieldwork is carried out. Even though she produced a detailed compendium of possible dangers, Howell focuses particular attention on a limited number of major hazards: hepatitis, malaria, and vehicle accidents. In terms of their incidence and impact, each poses major problems for anthropologists; but the risks from each are capable of being reduced, provided proper attention is paid to their prevention and possible remedy.

The hazards faced by researchers in Western urban environments are perhaps less striking than those that confront anthropologists. At least the former are spared the problems of disease and of obtaining assistance over long distances or in difficult terrain found in remote regions. Nevertheless, ethnography in the urban West is not without its hazards. Research among those designated earlier as gangs and outlaws seems to pose particular problems. Researchers who have worked with such groups report that violence is not unusual, frequently forceful, and often unexpected. Research in situations of violent social conflict or on drug abuse, on the other hand, poses fewer problems than might appear at first; although, especially in conflict situations, the identity of the researcher has crucial consequences for how far he or she is accepted within the setting. Discussion of the dangers facing female researchers has latterly become more open. There remains a clear need for the issues raised by the sexual harassment and sexual assault of female researchers to be discussed more widely.

The social meanings of danger are subculturally specific. In hazardous occupations like law enforcement, danger is seen as a source of excitement, which differentiates the occupation from others and serves as a relief from an otherwise boring routine (Fielding, 1988). Among the skydivers studied by Lyng (1990; Lyng & Snow, 1986) danger was variously defined in hedonistic, countercultural, and "edgework" terms. (The term *edgework* refers an individual's ability to test the limits of control over life-and-death situations through a fusion of personal qualities and technical skills.) The social meanings of danger in ethnographic research have been articulated in contradictory ways. They have sometimes been suffused by a romanticism that expresses, as Gouldner (1968) puts it, "the satisfaction of the Great White Hunter who has bravely risked the perils of the [urban] jungle to bring back an exotic specimen" (p. 107). Conversely, social scientists have also been sometimes too ready to accept at face value media definitions of the dangers allegedly to be found in particular settings. In doing so, researchers make life easy for themselves. As Barnes (1984) points out, data collection and analysis run more smoothly in areas of social life characterized by consensus rather than conflict. Yet, areas of conflict are precisely those where research is generally seen as having an important relevance to wider societal concerns. Hence, as Barnes (1984) observes, "we have the paradox that the more we are able to speak with professional competence or confidence, the less important it is that anyone should listen to what we have to say" (pp. 102-103). Neither timidity nor a romantic denial of the dangers posed by fieldwork serves us well.

REFERENCES

Ackers, H. L. (1993). Racism, sexuality and the process of ethnographic research. In D. Hobbs & T. May (Eds.), *Interpreting the field: Accounts of ethnography*. Oxford: Clarendon.

Adler, P. A. (1985). *Wheeling and dealing: An ethnography of an upper-level drug dealing and smuggling community*. New York: Columbia University Press.

Adler, P. A., & Adler, P. (1987). *Membership roles in field research*. Newbury Park, CA: Sage.

Adler, P. A., & Adler, P. (1991). Stability and flexibility: Maintaining relations with organized and unorganized groups. In W. B. Shaffir & R. A. Stebbins (Eds.), *Experiencing fieldwork: An inside view of qualitative research*. Newbury Park, CA: Sage.

Adler, P. A., & Adler, P. (1993). Ethical issues in self-censorship: Ethnographic research on sensitive topics. In C. M. Renzetti & R. M. Lee (Eds.), *Researching sensitive topics*. Newbury Park, CA: Sage.

Agar, M. (1969). The simulated situation: A methodological note. *Human Organization, 28*, 322-329.

Alevy, D. J., Bunker, B. B., Doob, L. J., Foltz, W. J., French, N., Klein, E. B., & Miller, J. C. (1974). Rationale, research and role relations in the Stirling workshop. *Journal of Conflict Resolution, 18*, 276-284.

Anderson, L., & Calhoun, T. C. (1992). Facilitative aspects of field research with deviant street populations. *Sociological Inquiry, 62*, 490-498.

Argyris, C. (1952). Diagnosing defenses against the outsider. *Journal of Social Issues, 8*, 24-34.

Armstrong, G. (1993). Like that Desmond Morris? In D. Hobbs & T. May (Eds.), *Interpreting the field: Accounts of ethnography*. Oxford: Clarendon.

Barnes, J. A. (1979). *Who should know what? Social science, privacy and ethics*. Harmondsworth, UK: Penguin.

Barnes, J. A. (1984). Ethical and political compromises in social research. *Wisconsin Sociologist, 21*, 100-110.

Beals, R. L. (1969). *Politics of social research: An inquiry into the ethics and responsibilities of social scientists*. Chicago: Aldine.

Bell, C. (1984). The SSRC: Restructured and defended. In C. Bell & H. Roberts (Eds.), *Social researching: Politics, problems, practice*. London: Routledge & Kegan Paul.

Berk, R. A., & Adams, J. M. (1970). Establishing rapport with deviant groups. *Social Problems, 18*, 102-117.

Bettelheim, B. (1961). *The informed heart: The human condition in modern mass society*. London: Thames & Hudson.

Beynon, H. (1988). Regulating research: Politics and decision making in industrial organizations. In A. Bryman (Ed.), *Doing research on organizations*. London: Routledge.

Biernacki, P., & Waldorf, D. (1981). Snowball sampling: Problems and techniques of chain referral sampling. *Sociological Methods and Research, 10*, 141-163.

Boas, F. (1919). Scientists as spies. *The Nation, 109*, p. 793.

Boehringer, G., Zeroulis, V., Bayley, J., & Boehringer, R. (1974). Stirling: The destructive application of group techniques. *Journal of Conflict Resolution, 18*, 257-275.

Bourgois, P. (1989). In search of Horatio Alger: Culture and ideology in the crack economy. *Contemporary Drug Problems, 16*, 619-649.

Bourgois, P. (1990). Confronting anthropological ethics: Ethnographic lessons from Central America. *Journal of Peace Research, 27*, 43-54.

Bowman, G. (1993). Nationalizing the sacred: Shrines and shifting identities in the Israeli-occupied territories. *Man: The Journal of the Royal Anthropological Institute, 28*(3), 431-460.

Brahuja, M., & Hallowell, L. (1986). Legal intrusion and the politics of fieldwork: The impact of the Brahuja case. *Urban Life, 14*, 454-478.

Brannen, J. (1988). The study of sensitive subjects. *Sociological Review, 36*, 552-563.

Brewer, J. D. (1991). *Inside the RUC: Routine policing in a divided society.* Oxford: Oxford University Press.

Brewer, J. D. (1993). Sensitivity as a problem in field research: A study of routine policing in Northern Ireland. In C. M. Renzetti & R. M. Lee (Eds.), *Researching sensitive topics.* Newbury Park, CA: Sage.

Broadhead, R. S., & Fox, K. J. (1990). Takin' it to the streets: AIDS outreach as ethnography. *Journal of Contemporary Ethnography, 19*, 322-348.

Bromley, D. G., & Shupe, A. D., Jr. (1980). Evolving foci in participant observation: Research as an emergent process. In W. B. Shaffir, R. A. Stebbins, & A. Turowetz (Eds.), *Fieldwork experience: Qualitative approaches to social research.* New York: St. Martin's Press.

Brown, R., Bute, S., & Ford, P. (1986). *Social workers at risk: The prevention and management of violence.* London: Macmillan.

Bruce, S. (1987). Gullibles travels: The native sociologist. In N. McKeganey & S. Cunningham-Burley (Eds.), *Enter the sociologist: Reflections on the practice of sociology.* Aldershot, UK: Avebury.

Bruce, S. (1992). *The red hand: Protestant paramilitaries in Northern Ireland.* Oxford: Oxford University Press.

Bufwack, M. A. (1975). *Village without violence: An examination of a Northern Irish village.* Unpublished doctoral dissertation, Washington University, St. Louis, MO.

Bulmer, M. (1982a). Ethical problems in social research: The case of covert participant observation. In M. Bulmer (Ed.), *Social research ethics.* London: Macmillan.

Bulmer, M. (1982b). The research ethics of pseudo-patient studies: A new look at the merits of covert ethnographic methods. *Sociological Review, 30*, 628-648.

Burton, F. (1978). *The politics of legitimacy: Struggle in a Belfast community.* London: Routledge & Kegan Paul.

Carey, J. T. (1972). Problems of access and risk in observing drug scenes. In J. D. Douglas (Ed.), *Research on deviance.* New York: Random House.

Cohen, S. (1972). *Folk devils and moral panics: The creation of the mods and the rockers.* London: McGibbon & Kee.

Corsino, L. (1987). Fieldworker blues: Emotional stress and research underinvolvement in fieldwork settings. *Social Science Journal, 24*, 275-285.

Crookall, D., Oxford, R., & Saunders, D. (1987). Towards a reconceptualization of simulations: From representation to reality. *Simulation/Games for Learning, 17*, 147-171.

Curtis, L. (1984). *Ireland and the propaganda war: The British media and the battle for hearts and minds.* London: Pluto Press.

CVCP. (1993). *Health and safety responsibilities of supervisors towards postgraduate and undergraduate students.* London: Committee of Vice-Chancellors and Principals of the Universities of the United Kingdom.

Daniels, A. K. (1967). The low-caste stranger in social research. In G. Sjoberg (Ed.), *Ethics, politics and social research.* London: Routledge & Kegan Paul.

Davidowicz, L. S. (1981). *The holocaust and the historians.* Cambridge, MA: Harvard University Press.

Davison, C., Frankel, S., & Smith, G. D. (1992). To hell with tommorow: Coronary heart disease and the ethnography of fatalism. In S. Scott, G. Williams, S. Platt, & H. Thomas (Eds.), *Private risks and public dangers.* Aldershot, UK: Avebury.

De Pres, T. (1976). *The survivor: An anatomy of life in the death camps.* New York: Oxford University Press.

Diamond, S. (1964). Nigerian discovery: The politics of field work. In A. J. Vidich, J. Bensman, & M. R. Stein (Eds.), *Reflections on community studies.* New York: Harper & Row.

Doob, L. J., & Foltz, W. F. (1973). The Belfast workshop: An application of group techniques to a destructive conflict. *Journal of Conflict Resolution, 17,* 489-512.

Doob, L. J., & Foltz, W. F. (1974). The impact of a workshop upon grass-roots leaders in Belfast. *Journal of Conflict Resolution, 18,* 237-256.

Douglas, D. (1972). Managing fronts in observing deviance. In J. D. Douglas (Ed.), *Research on deviance.* New York: Random House.

Douglas, J. D. (1976). *Investigative social research: Individual and team field research.* Beverly Hills, CA: Sage.

Dumont, J-P. (1992). Ideas on Philippine violence: Assertions, negations and narrations. In C. Nordstom & J-A. Martin (Eds.), *The paths to domination, resistance and terror.* Berkeley: University of California Press.

Easterday, L., Papademas, D., Schorr, L., & Valentine, C. (1977). The making of a female researcher: Role problems in fieldwork. *Urban Life, 6,* 333-348.

Ekker, K., Gifford, G., Leik, S. A., & Leik, R. A. (1988). Using microcomputer game-simulation experiments to study family response to the Mt. St. Helens' eruptions. *Social Science Computer Review, 6,* 90-105.

Ellen, R. F. (Ed.). (1984). *Ethnographic research: A guide to general conduct.* London: Academic Press.

Faligot, R. (1983). *Britain's military strategy in Northern Ireland: The Kitson experiment.* London: Zed Press.

Feldman, A. (1991). *Formations of violence: The narrative of the body and political terror in Northern Ireland.* Chicago: Chicago University Press.

Fielding, N. (1982). Observational research on the national front. In M. Bulmer (Eds.), *Social research ethics.* London: Macmillan.

Fielding, N. G. (1988). *Joining forces.* London: Routledge.

Fischer, C. F. (1972). Observing a crowd: The structure and description of protest demonstrations. In J. D. Douglas (Ed.), *Research on deviance.* New York: Random House.

Fitzpatrick, J. S. (1980). Adapting to danger: A participant observation study of an underground mine. *Sociology of Work and Occupations, 7,* 131-158.

Fountain, J. (1993). Dealing with data. In D. Hobbs & T. May (Eds.), *Interpreting the field: Accounts of ethnography.* Oxford: Clarendon.

Fox, K. J. (1991). The politics of prevention: Ethnographers combat AIDS among drug users. In M. Burawoy, A. Burton, A. A. Ferguson, K. J. Fox, J. Gamson, N. Gartrell, L. Hurst, C. Kurzman, L. Salinger, J. Schiffman, & S. Ui (Eds.), *Ethnography unbound: Power and resistance in the modern metropolis.* Berkeley: University of California Press.

Gallmeier, C. P. (1991). Leaving, revisiting and staying in touch: Neglected issues in field research. In W. B. Shaffir & R. A. Stebbins (Eds.), *Experiencing fieldwork: An inside view of qualitative research.* Newbury Park, CA: Sage.

Gambetta, D. (1993). *The Sicilian Mafia: The business of private protection.* Cambridge, MA: Harvard University Press.

Gilmore, D. D. (1991). Subjectivity and subjugation: Fieldwork in the stratified community. *Human Organization, 50,* 215-224.

Glaser, B. G., & Strauss, A. L. (1967). *The discovery of grounded theory.* Chicago: Aldine.

Glazer, M. (1966). Fieldwork in a hostile environment: A chapter in the sociology of social research in Chile. *Comparative Education Review, 10*(2), 367-376.

Goffman, E. (1961). *Asylums: Essays on the social situation of mental patients and other inmates.* New York: Anchor.

Goffman, E. (1970). *Strategic interaction.* Oxford: Basil Blackwell.

Goffman, E. (1971). *Relations in public: Microstudies of the public order.* New York: Harper & Row.

Goffman, E. (1977). Where the action is. In E. Goffman, *Interaction ritual.* Harmondsworth, UK: Penguin.

Golde, P. (1986). *Women in the field* (2nd ed.). Berkeley: University of California Press.

Gouldner, A. W. (1954). *Patterns of industrial bureaucracy.* Glencoe, IL: Free Press.

Gouldner, A. W. (1968). The sociologist as partisan. *American Sociologist, 3,* 103-116.

Green, J. (1992). Some problems in the development of a sociology of accidents. In S. Scott, G. Williams, S. Platt, & H. Thomas (Eds.), *Private risks and public dangers.* Aldershot, UK: Avebury.

Greer, S. (1988). The supergrass system. In A. Jennings (Ed.), *Justice under fire: The abuse of civil liberties in Northern Ireland.* London: Pluto Press.

Griffiths, S. (1993, October 15). Don among the dons. *The Times Higher Education Supplement,* p. 40.

Gurney, J. N. (1985). Not one of the guys: The female researcher in a male-dominated setting. *Qualitative Sociology, 8,* 42-62.

Gurney, J. N. (1991). Female researchers in male-dominated settings: Implications for short-term versus long-term research. In W. B. Shaffir & R. A. Stebbins (Eds.), *Experiencing fieldwork: An inside view of qualitative research.* Newbury Park, CA: Sage.

Haas, J. (1977). Learning real feelings: A study of high steel ironworkers' reactions to fear and danger. *Sociology of Work and Occupations, 4,* 147-170.

Haney, C., Curtis, B., & Zimbardo, P. G. (1973). Interpersonal dynamics in a simulated prison. *International Journal of Criminology and Penology, 1,* 69-97.

Henslin, J. M. (1972). Studying deviance in four settings: Research experiences with cabbies, suicides, drug users and abortionees. In J. D. Douglas (Ed.), *Research on deviance.* New York: Random House.

Heskin, K. (1980). *Northern Ireland: A psychological analysis.* Dublin: Gill & Macmillan.

Hill, B. J. (1982). An analysis of conflict resolution techniques: From problem solving workshops to theory. *Journal of Conflict Resolution, 26*, 109-138.

Hillyard, P. (1988). Political and social dimensions of emergency law in Northern Ireland. In A. Jennings (Ed.), *Justice under fire: The abuse of civil liberties in Northern Ireland*. London: Pluto Press.

Hopper, C. B., & Moore, J. (1990). Women in outlaw motorcycle gangs. *Journal of Contemporary Ethnography, 18*, 363-387.

Horowitz, I. L. (1967). Project Camelot: Selected reactions and personal reflections. In G. Sjoberg (Ed.), *Ethics, politics and social research*. London: Routledge & Kegan Paul.

Horowitz, R. (1986). Remaining an outsider: Membership as a threat to research rapport. *Urban Life, 14*, 409-430.

Howell, N. (1990). *Surviving fieldwork: A report of the advisory panel on health and safety in fieldwork*. Washington, DC: American Anthropological Association.

Humphreys, L. (1970). *Tearoom trade: A study of homosexual encounters in public places*. London: Duckworth.

Hunt, J. C. (1989). *Psychoanalytic aspects of fieldwork*. Newbury Park, CA: Sage.

Husarska, A. (1992, October 5). Annals of journalism: News from hell. *The New Yorker*, pp. 89-104.

Hyatt, M. (1990). *Franz Boas social activist: The dynamics of ethnicity*. New York: Greenwood.

Inciardi, J. (1993). Some considerations on the methods, dangers and ethics of crack-house research. In J. A. Inciardi, D. Lockwood, & A. E. Pottinger, *Women and crack-cocaine*. New York: Macmillan.

Jankowski, M. S. (1991). *Islands in the street: Gangs and American urban society*. Berkeley: University of California Press.

Jenkins, R. (1983). *Lads, citizens and ordinary kids*. London: Routledge & Kegan Paul.

Jenkins, R. (1984). Bringing it all back home: An anthropologist in Belfast. In C. Bell & H. Roberts (Eds.), *Social researching: Politics, problems, practice*. London: Routledge & Kegan Paul.

Johnson, B. D., Goldstein, P. J., Preble, E., Schmeidler, J., Lipton, D. S., Spunt, B., & Miller, T. (1985). *Taking care of business: The economics of crime by heroin abusers*. Lexington, MA: D. C. Heath.

Johnson, J. (1975). *Doing field research*. New York: Free Press.

Johnson, L. K. (1989). *America's secret power: The CIA in a democratic society*. New York: Oxford University Press.

Kanter, R. M. (1977). *Men and women of the corporation*. New York: Basic Books.

Kidron, M., & Smith, D. (1991). *The new state of war and peace: An international atlas*. London: Grafton Books.

Klatch, R. E. (1988). The methodological problems of studying a politically resistant community. In R. G. Burgess (Ed.), *Studies in qualitative methodology: Vol. 1. Conducting qualitative research*. Greenwich, CT: JAI.

Kleinman, S. (1991). Field-workers' feelings: What we feel, who we are, how we analyze. In W. B. Shaffir & R. B. Stebbins (Eds.), *Experiencing fieldwork: An inside view of qualitative research*. Newbury Park, CA: Sage.

Knerr, C. R. (1982). What to do before and after a subpoena of data arrives. In J. E. Seiber (Ed.), *The ethics of social research: Vol. 1. Surveys and experiments*. New York: Springer-Verlag.

Kotarba, J. (1990). Ethnography and AIDS: Returning to the streets. *Journal of Contemporary Ethnography, 19,* 259-270.

Kulick, D. (1991). Law and order in Papua New Guinea. *Anthropology Today, 7*(5), 21-22.

Lee, R., & Hurlich, S. (1982). From foragers to fighters: South Africa's militarization of the Namibian San. In E. Leacock & R. Lee (Eds.), *Politics and history in band society.* Cambridge, UK: Cambridge University Press.

Lee, R. M. (1992). Nobody said it had to be easy: Postgraduate field research in Northern Ireland. In R. G. Burgess (Ed.), *Studies in qualitative methodology: Vol. 3. Learning about fieldwork.* Greenwich, CT: JAI.

Lee, R. M. (1993). *Doing research on sensitive topics.* London: Sage.

Leonard, M. (1993, April). *Informal work and employment in Belfast: Researching a sensitive topic in a politically sensitive locality.* Paper presented at Annual Conference of the British Sociological Association, University of Essex.

Lipset, D. (1993). Law and order in Papua New Guinea. *Anthropology Today, 9*(6), 18.

Lockwood, J. (1982). Conducting research in Northern Ireland: A personal view. In P. Stringer (Ed.), *Confronting social issues: Vol. 2. Applications of social psychology.* London: Academic Press.

Lofland, J., & Lofland, L. H. (1984). *Analyzing social settings: A guide to qualitative observation and analysis.* Belmont, CA: Wadsworth.

Lutkehaus, N. (1986). She was very Cambridge: Camilla Wedgwood and the history of women in British social anthropology. *American Ethnologist, 13,* 776-798.

Lyng, S. (1990). Edgework: A social psychological analysis of voluntary risk taking. *American Journal of Sociology, 95*(4), 851-886.

Lyng, S. G., & Snow, D. A. (1986). Vocabularies of motive and high-risk behavior: The case of skydiving. In E. J. Lawler (Ed.), *Advances in group processes* (pp. 157-179). Greenwich, CT: JAI.

Manning, P. K. (1972). Observing the police: Deviants, resepectables and the law. In J. D. Douglas (Ed.), *Research on deviance.* New York: Random House.

Marx, G. T. (1988). *Undercover: Police surveillance in America.* Berkeley: University of California Press.

Matza, D. (1969). *Becoming deviant.* Englewood Cliffs, NJ: Prentice Hall.

Mayer, E. (1991). Peru in deep trouble: Mario Vargas Llosa's "Inquest in the Andes" reexamined. *Cultural Anthropology, 6,* 466-504.

McFarlane, G. (1986). Violence in rural Northern Ireland: Social scientific models, folk explanations and local variation? In D. Riches (Ed.), *The anthropology of violence.* Oxford: Basil Blackwell.

McFarlane, W. G. (1979). Mixed marriages in Ballycuan, Northern Ireland. *Journal of Comparative Family Studies, 10,* 191-205.

McKee, L., & O'Brien, M. (1983). Interviewing men: Taking gender seriously. In E. Gamarnikow, D. Morgan, J. Purvis, & D. Taylorson (Eds.), *The public and the private.* London: Heinemann.

McKeganey, N. (1990). Drug abuse in the community: Needle-sharing and the risks of HIV infection. In S. Cunningham-Burley & N. McKeganey (Eds.), *Readings in medical sociology.* London: Routledge.

McNamara, J. K. (1987). Taking sides in conflict: Applied social research in the South African gold-mining industry. In G. C. Wenger (Ed.), *The research relationship: Practice and politics in social policy research.* London: Allen & Unwin.

Migdal, J. S. (1979). *Palestinian society and politics.* Princeton, NJ: Princeton University Press.

Milroy, L. (1980). *Language and social networks.* Oxford: Basil Blackwell.

Mitchell, R. G. (1983). *Mountain experience: The psychology and sociology of adventure.* Chicago: University of Chicago Press.

Mitchell, R. G., Jr. (1991). Secrecy and disclosure in fieldwork. In W. B. Shaffir & R. A. Stebbins (Eds.), *Experiencing fieldwork: An inside view of qualitative research.* Newbury Park, CA: Sage.

Moore, R. (1971). Becoming a sociologist in Sparkbrook. In C. Bell & H. Newby (Eds.), *Doing sociological research.* London: Allen & Unwin.

Morgan, D. H. J. (1972). The British association scandal: The effect of publicity on sociological investigation. *Sociological Review, 20,* 185-206.

Murphy, M. D. (1985). Rumors of identity: Gossip and rapport in ethnographic research. *Human Organization, 44,* 132-137.

Nader, L. (1986). From anguish to exultation. In P. Golde (Ed.), *Women in the field: Anthropological experiences.* Berkeley: University of California Press.

Nakhleh, K. (1979). On being a native anthropologist. In G. Huizer & B. Mannheim (Eds.), *The politics of anthropology: From colonialism and sexism toward a view from below.* The Hague: Mouton.

Nash, J. (1979). Ethnology in a revolutionary setting. In G. Huizer & B. Mannheim (Eds.), *The politics of anthropology: From colonialism and sexism toward a view from below.* The Hague: Mouton.

Nelson, R. L., & Hedrick, T. E. (1983). The statutory protection of confidential research data: Synthesis and evaluation. In R. F. Boruch & J. S. Cecil (Eds.), *Solutions to ethical and legal problems in social research.* New York: Academic Press.

Noone, R. (1972). *Rape of the dream people.* London: Hutchinson.

Nordstom, C., & Martin, J. (1992). The culture of conflict: Field reality and theory. In C. Nordstom & J. Martin (Eds.), *The paths to domination, resistance and terror.* Berkeley: University of California Press.

Norris, D. (1990). *Violence against social workers: The implications for practice.* London: Jessica Kingsley.

O'Dowd, L. (1986). Ignoring the communal divide: The implications for social research. In R. Jenkins (Ed.), *Northern Ireland: Studies in economic and social life.* Aldershot, UK: Avebury.

Obbo, C. (1990). Adventures with fieldnotes. In R. Sanjek (Ed.), *Fieldnotes: The making of anthropology.* Ithaca, NY: Cornell University Press.

Patrick, J. (1973). *A Glasgow gang observed.* London: Eyre Methuen.

Patton, M. Q. (1987). *How to use qualitative methods in evaluation.* Newbury Park, CA: Sage.

Pepinsky, H. E. (1980). A sociologist on police patrol. In W. B. Shaffir, R. A. Stebbins, & A. Turowetz (Eds.), *Fieldwork experiences: Qualitative approaches to social research.* New York: St. Martin's Press.

Peritore, N. P. (1990). Reflections on dangerous fieldwork. *American Sociologist, 21,* 359-372.

Pollner, M., & Emerson, R. M. (1983). The dynamics of inclusion and distance in fieldwork relations. In R. M. Emerson (Ed.), *Contemporary field research: A collection of readings.* Boston: Little, Brown.

Polsky, N. (1971). *Hustlers, beats and others.* Harmondsworth, UK: Penguin.

Power, R. (1989). Participant observation and its place in the study of illicit drug abuse. *British Journal of Addiction, 84,* 43-52.

Power, R. (1993, April). *Ethical issues in employing drug users in community-based research.* Paper presented at the Conference of the British Sociological Association, University of Essex.

Punch, M. (1979). *Policing the inner city: A study of Amsterdam's Warmoesstraat.* London: Macmillan.

Reinharz, S. (1979). *On becoming a social scientist.* San Francisco: Jossey-Bass.

Reiss, A. J., Jr. (1979). Governmental regulation of scientific inquiry: Some paradoxical consequences. In C. B. Klockars & F. W. O'Connor (Eds.), *Deviance and decency: The ethics of research with human subjects.* Beverly Hills, CA: Sage.

Richelson, J. (1985). *The U.S. intelligence community.* Cambridge, MA: Ballinger.

Rossi, P. H., & Freeman, H. E. (1982). *Evaluation: A systematic approach.* Beverly Hills, CA: Sage.

Roth, J. A. (1966). Hired hand research. *American Sociologist, 1,* 190-196.

Roy, D. (1970). The study of southern labor union organizing campaigns. In R. W. Habenstein (Ed.), *Pathways to data.* Chicago: Aldine.

Schwartz, B. (1970). Notes on the sociology of sleep. *Sociological Quarterly, 11,* 458-499.

Shapiro, S. P. (1987). The social control of impersonal trust. *American Journal of Sociology, 93,* 623-658.

Sjoberg, G., & Nett, R. (1968). *A methodology for social research.* New York: Harper & Row.

Sluka, J. A. (1990). Participant observation in violent social contexts. *Human Organization, 49,* 114-126.

Small, S. (1983). *Police and people in London: II. A group of black young people.* London: Policy Studies Institute.

Smith, H. W. (1975). *Strategies of social research: The methodological imagination.* London: Prentice Hall.

Spector, M. (1980). Learning to study public figures. In W. B. Shaffir, R. A. Stebbins, & A. Turowetz (Eds.), *Fieldwork experience: Qualitative approaches to social research.* New York: St. Martin's Press.

Spencer, G. (1973). Methodological issues in the study of bureaucratic élites: A case study of West Point. *Social Problems, 21,* 90-103.

Stanko, E. A. (1992). Intimidating education: Sexual harassment in criminology. *Journal of Criminal Justice Education, 3,* 331-340.

Starn, O. (1991). Missing the revolution: Anthropologists and the war in Peru. *Cultural Anthropology, 6,* 63-91.

Stephenson, R. M. (1978). The CIA and the professor: A personal account. *American Sociologist, 13,* 128-133.

Taylor, R. (1986). *The Queens University of Belfast and its relationship to the troubles.* Doctoral thesis, University of Kent at Canterbury.

Teeman, A. (1993, January 15). Geology on the rocks. *The Times Higher Education Supplement,* p. 5.

Thorne, B. (1983). Political activist as participant observer: Conflicts of commitment in a study of the draft resistance movement in the 1960s. In R. M. Emerson (Ed.), *Contemporary field research: A collection of readings.* Boston: Little, Brown.

University of Toronto. (1988). *University of Toronto policy for safety in field research.* Toronto: University of Toronto, Office of the Vice President–Research.

Van den Berghe, P. L. (1967). Research in South Africa: The story of my experiences with tyranny. In G. Sjoberg (Ed.), *Ethics, politics and social research.* London: Routledge & Kegan Paul.

Van Maanen, J. (1988). *Tales of the field.* Chicago: University of Chicago Press.

Van Maanen, J. (1991). Playing back the tape: Early days in the field. In W. B. Shaffir & R. A. Stebbins (Eds.), *Experiencing fieldwork: An inside view of qualitative research.* Newbury Park, CA: Sage.

Van Ments, M. (1983). *The effective use of role-play.* London: Kogan Page.

Wakin, E. (1992). *Anthropology goes to war: Professional ethics and counterinsurgency in Thailand.* Madison: University of Wisconsin Center for Southeast Asian Studies.

Walford, G. (1987). Research role conflicts and compromises in public schools. In G. Walford (Ed.), *Doing sociology of education.* London: Falmer Press.

Walker, A. L., & Lidz, C. W. (1977). Methodological notes on the employment of indigenous observers. In R. S. Weppner (Ed.), *Street ethnography.* Beverly Hills, CA: Sage.

Warren, C. A. B. (1988). *Gender issues in field research.* Newbury Park, CA: Sage.

Wax, R. H. (1971). *Doing fieldwork: Warnings and advice.* Chicago: University of Chicago Press.

Weaver, T. (Ed.). (1973). *To see ourselves: Anthropology and modern social issues.* Glenview, IL: Scott, Foresman.

Whitehead, T. L., & Price, L. (1986). Summary: Sex and the fieldwork experience. In T. L. Whitehead & M. E. Conaway (Eds.), *Self, sex, and gender in cross-cultural fieldwork.* Urbana: University of Illinois Press.

Williams, T., Dunlap, E., Johnson, B. D., & Hamid, A. (1992). Personal safety in dangerous places. *Journal of Contemporary Ethnography, 21,* 343-374.

Wilson, G. K., & Wallensteen, P. (1988). Major armed conflicts in 1987. In Stockholm International Peace Research Institute Institute, *World armaments and disarmament.* Oxford: Oxford University Press.

Wintrob, R. M. (1969). Stress and response in fieldwork. In F. Henry & S. Saberwal (Eds.), *Stress and response in fieldwork.* New York: Holt, Rinehart & Winston.

Wojtas, O. (1994, January 28). Hunters sabotaged research. *The Times Higher Education Supplement,* p. 3.

Wolf, D. R. (1991). High-risk methodology: Reflections on leaving an outlaw society. In W. B. Shaffir & R. A. Stebbins (Eds.), *Experiencing fieldwork: An inside view of qualitative research.* Newbury Park, CA: Sage.

Wood, S. (1980). *Reactions to redundancy.* Unpublished doctoral thesis, University of Manchester, UK.

Yancey, W. L., & Rainwater, L. (1970). Problems in the ethnography of the urban underclasses. In R. W. Habenstein (Ed.), *Pathways to data.* Chicago: Aldine.

Zimbardo, P. G. (1973). On the ethics of intervention in human psychological research: With special reference to the Stanford prison experiment. *Cognition, 2,* 243-256.

Zulaika, J. (1988). *Basque violence: Metaphor and sacrament.* Reno: University of Nevada Press.

ABOUT THE AUTHOR

RAYMOND M. LEE is Lecturer in Social Research Methods in the Department of Social Policy and Social Science, Royal Holloway University of London. He has a background in both survey research and field methods, and his main research interests are in research methodology, the sociology of labor markets, and the sociology of religion. His most recent work has been concerned with the methodological problems and issues associated with research on sensitive topics and with the impact of new technologies on research methods in the social sciences. He is the author of *Doing Research on Sensitive Topics,* and has edited *Researching Sensitive Topics* (with Claire Renzetti) and *Using Computers in Qualitative Research* (with Nigel Fielding), all of which are published by Sage.